CAMDEN STORIES OF SERVICE IN WORLD WAR II

Janice Johnson

Camden Historical Society

Published by the Camden Historical Society Inc.
40 John Street, Camden, NSW 2570.
(SAN: 908-3022)

www.camdenhistory.org.au

Published with funds from the Estate of the late Janice Johnson, who died in 2017.

© 2021 by the Camden Historical Society Inc.

All rights reserved. No part of this publication may be used or reproduced in any manner whatsoever without written permission, except in the case of brief quotations in critical articles and reviews. For more information, contact the Camden Historical Society PO Box 566 Camden NSW 2570 Australia. (secretary@camdenhistory.org.au)

The copyright duration has passed on the included newspaper quotations. These quotations are not subject to this copyright claim.

First edition published in 2021.

ISBN: 978-0-6485894-4-0

Front Cover: Corporal John Edmondson of the 2/17 Battalion, AIF - from the Australian War Memorial - accession number is P00426.003.

Back Cover: A copy of a Certificate of Appreciation presented to Sergeant Jack Dunk (NX32715) by the Parishioners of St John's Church, Camden.

Contents

Contents	iii
Illustrations	vii
Introduction – Camden Historical Society	ix
War in Europe	1
Bate, Henry Jefferson Percival (Jeff)	5
Clark, James	9
Downes, Rupert Frederick Arding (Derick)	10
Edmondson, John Hurst	11
Healy, James	14
Kartzoff, Michel Eugene (Mike)	15
Marriott, Lewis (Lew) Charles	17
McLeod, Gordon John	22
Mundell, William (Bill)	23
Tate, Colin	25
Wills, Leonard Suttor	26
War in the Mediterranean and the Middle East	27
Davis, Edward Allen	28
Evans, William Allan	29
McGrath, Ernest Henry	30
Williams, Errol Wallis Stevenson	32
Williams, Major	34
Woollams, Frederick Charles	36
War in the Pacific	37
Booth, Edward James	39
Carling, Francis	41
Chesham, Harold Charles	42
Crookston, Jacqueline	43
Gander, Horace Arthur	44

Smart, Harold William	45
On the Home Front	**47**
Italian youths gaoled	49
Baron Frederick Elliott von Frankenberg	49
Macarthur-Onslow, Andrew William	51
Wilkinson nee Malcolm, Doreen Grace	53
Sidman, Marie Celeste	54
Weir, Jean	56
Prisoners of War	**59**
Payten, David Rose	60
Wheatley, Max Ian	61
Boyd, James William	63
Chapman, Arthur William	65
Donaldson, Neil	66
Fallon, Harold Augustus (Bill)	67
Gunn, Francis Orchard	68
Kelloway, Eric George	69
Rapley, Edwin Morton	70
Skene, Charles Robertson (Bob)	71
Segal, Norman Evan	72
Skinner, Amos Richard	73
Merchant Navy	**74**
French, Henry Bernard (Barney)	75
Kent, George Joseph	76
Mundle, George Valentine	77
Starr, Mervyn Joseph	78
Varlow, Charles Kingsley	79
War's End	**83**

Welcome Home	85
Eric George Kelloway	87
Edwin Morton Rapley	87
McKnight, Keith	88
Doust, Lyle	89
Evans, Ivor Morgan	90
Pratt, Kenneth Scott	91
Pratt, Jean Kinnear	92
Pratt, John	93
Hickey, Marjorie Wanda	95
Editors' comments	96
Index	97
Awards	97
Diseases	97
Other	97
People	97
Places	103
Units	105
Bibliography	107

Illustrations

Booth, Edward	39
Boyd, James William	63
Carling, Francis	41
Clark, James	9
Crookston, Jacqueline	43
Edmondson V.C., John	11
Frankenberg, Baron Frederick Elliot von	49
Gander, Horace	44
Gowrie, His Excellency the Right Honourable Lord	38
Johnson, Janice	ix
Kooringa, Merchant Navy Ship	76
Macarthur-Onslow, Andrew	51
Marriott, Lewis	17
McLeod, Gordon John	22
Mundell, William	23
Tate, Colin	25
Williams, Errol & Major	33
Williams, Major	34
Williams, Major – The grave of Major	35
Wilkinson nee Malcolm, Doreen	53
Weir, Jean	57

Introduction – Camden Historical Society

A local newspaper reflects the values and attitudes of the community at the time. During World War II, the *Camden News* revealed the Camden community's values. It conveyed the strong sense of community of those days in Camden when everyone knew everyone else or was related to everyone else. The newspaper was providing a service to its readers by sharing interesting information. It was also contributing to community identity and a sense of place.

Janice Johnson has gathered the paper's articles about the Camden servicemen and women engaged in the war. It is possible to see the patriotic enthusiasm as the war started and the proud farewells to the young men going off to war. Later there are more sombre accounts of prisoners of war, injuries, and deaths. This book tells us our history, but this is through the participants' writings and opinions at the time.

Janice Johnson

The strong patriotism of the *Camden News* editor, William Sidman, guided him to select and give preference to some stories and suppress others. Occasionally he inserts a personal note in the paper, e.g., 6 March 1941: [*Letters from boys at the front are most interesting to their friends; pass the news on to them through 'The Camden News'.*]

The book focuses squarely on the printed articles which were in the *Camden News*. These are available through the wonderful resource *Trove*, https://trove.nla.gov.au/newspaper/, but Janice inserts the information from the National Archives of Australia https://recordsearch.naa.gov.au/ on World War II men and women. The book also includes some personal letters available only at the Camden Museum. Through the book, the poppy represents the death of a soldier.

Janice Johnson died in 2017, but she left money for the printing of this book. Janice had an ongoing interest in local studies and was a Camden Historical Society and Camden Family History Society member. She had a particular interest in the people and events that helped shape Camden.

She was the author or editor of:

- *Camden's WWI Diggers: 1914-1918*
- *Camden – Unlocking the Past* (Co-author with Brian Burnett)
- *Part 1 Pioneer and Federation Index* (e-Book)
- *Reminiscences Early Camden* (Editor)
- *Reflections on Old Sydney and Colonial Days* (Editor)
- *They Worked at Camden Park* (Co-author of 3rd, 4th, and 5th editions)
- *We Do But Sleep: The Cemeteries & Columbarium of the Camden & Menangle Anglican Parishes* (e-Book)
- *Camden Through a Poet's Eyes 1847 to 1854 – Charles Tompson (Jnr.)*
- *Camden Soldiers of King and Queen 1788 to 1913*

The Camden Historical Society pays tribute to her work as a researcher. Members of the Society have edited the book and made minor changes to help readers. The Editors' notes page at the end of the book outlines the changes and contains a guide on interpreting the information in Janice's book.

War in Europe

As part of the British Empire, Australia was among the first nations to declare war on Nazi Germany. Between 1939 and 1945, nearly one million Australian men and women served in what was going to be World War II. They fought in campaigns against the Axis powers across Europe, the Mediterranean and North Africa.

Camden News, Thursday 27 June 1940, page 1.

FAREWELL TO CAMDEN VOLUNTEERS
MEMBERS OF THE 7th DIVISION A.I.F.

Between 700 and 800 people of Camden and district accepted the opportunity to publicly bid farewell to local volunteers who are members of the 7th Division of the A.I.F., and who shortly expect to be leaving for overseas service. The spacious Agricultural Hall had been loaned for the occasion, and the gathering was held last Friday night.

The proceedings opened with the National Anthem, followed by community singing, to music supplied by Mrs. Kelloway's orchestra. A musical programme filled the first hour, during which the following artists took part, songs by Miss Violet Wheeler, Mr. Michael Brien, Mr. Will O'Neill, Master Philip Haylock; a recitation by the hon. secretary of the movement, the Rev. A. E. Putland; and tap dances by Misses Bonny Woods and Daphne Howlett.

The stage had been appropriately decorated with flags and shrubs, and the centre table made attractive with a bowl of flowers.

After inviting the men of the 7th Division to come on to the platform, the President of the Soldiers and Citizens' Association, Mr. W. S. Cruikshank, addressed the gathering and made reference to the formation of the association as a result of a public meeting held, in Camden, and outlined its objects, which briefly were to publicly farewell all men from Camden and its environs who leave to serve with the A.I.F. No man, said the President, will leave this district without being publicly farewelled and receive some token of the people's respect. The association will also endeavour to render every possible assistance to those men when they return home. The gathering to night is to say farewell to men of the 7th Division of the A.I.F.

Mr. Cruikshank expressed pleasure in seeing such a large gathering to bid farewell to those men, and he earnestly hoped it would not be long before we would be able to welcome them back again to Camden. We will then welcome them, not only as soldiers, but as liberators, liberators from the scourge of Nazism which had overtaken the world. It was not only a sense of loyalty which had prompted these men to offer themselves, but barbarism of Hitler and his hordes had shaken the very foundation of our beings, the ruthless machine gunning from aeroplanes of women and children refugees, the bombing of hospital ships, such happenings make us ask has man ceased to be human. These men of the 7th Division say that Hitler cannot get away with that, and as the Germans in the last war learned of the fighting qualities of the A.I.F., so they will learn again.

These men are going to fight for freedom, that freedom which we citizens of the British Empire have enjoyed for so long, and we could say if Germany wins this war that freedom is gone, and we shall never see it retrieved. We read that the Germans did their goose-step into Paris, but we hope it will not be long before they do the double march back to Berlin.

The Mayor of Camden, Ald. H. S. Kelloway, on behalf of the people of the district, congratulated the members of the A.I.F. on the steps they had taken, and expressed the hope that it would not be long before they returned as happy and robust as they appeared on the stage that evening, and assured them of the unstinted support of the people of the district whilst they were away. He said he knew they would do well, as inspired by the traditions of the First A.I.F., reinforced by the knowledge that the people of the Empire, Great Britain, Canada, Africa, India, New Zealand and Australasia, spoke with one voice and through one mouthpiece, that of Mr. Winston Churchill, in whom we here have the greatest confidence. The Mayor pledged the people of the Camden district to do all in their power to prove worthy of the sacrifice the volunteers were making, and as a pledge of their fidelity, asked the soldiers to accept, through him, the right hand of every man, woman and child of this community, and thereupon shook hands with each of the men before him.

Dr. R. M. Crookston, in addressing the gathering, said we have met here to-night with pride and some sorrow in our hearts, to say farewell to men of the 7th Division who are going to join their comrades overseas. These men have offered their lives in the service of their country, and of humanity in a fight for the preservation of all that is worthwhile in life — for freedom, for the simple rights of men and women; and for everything that means decency and honour among men. This is not only the greatest, but the most just war in all history. It is more than a war. It is a crusade. Perhaps these men have not thought much about these things. Perhaps they only know that their country calls and needs them, and that they are ready to answer and go. I have seen so many men now come to enlist that I know the look in their faces as they come through the door. It is a look of quiet, and sometimes almost shy pride; a look of new-found peace and determination. It is the look on a man's face that tells that his conscience is at rest. I have never yet examined a man for the Service without emotion that is sometimes hard enough to hide, and I have never let one go without wishing him God speed, and a safe return, and I never will.

It is behind the ranks of men such as these, continued Dr. Crookston, that the Governments of the world are sheltering; some of them already broken, cowering and afraid, some of them still carrying on. It is for those Governments and for us, the people for whom they have offered everything, to see that they are supplied with all they need, with the weapons and munitions of war, food, comforts, and all that a soldier must have. And it is for us, and the Governments for whom they fight, to see that as they return they shall come back to a world better worth living in, and to a peace that shall prove that their sacrifice has not been in vain. And if we fail in that, and if our Governments lag behind in their duty to equip and supply them — let any Government which fails in its duty to its men beware of the wrath of the people which will follow the war.

Major-General J. Macarthur Onslow assisted by Dr. R. M. Crookston, was called upon to make the presentation to each of the soldiers, such presentation consisting of an inscribed wallet with bullet proof mirror and a Commonwealth note, also a special bag of comforts provided by the Women's Voluntary Services. At the conclusion of the presentations supper was provided by the various women's organisations of the town, and dancing for the younger people was carried out until late at night.

A collection towards expenses realised over £20.

> The recipients were: —
> Qtr. Sergt. A. J. OLIVER ;
> Gunner R. HUGHES ;
> Gunner A. L. WHITELEY ;
> Gunner H. HAL ;
> Sapper George GOFF ;
> Gunner T. N. FILBY ;
> Gunner R. H. LARNACH ;
> Pte. K. C. LARNACH ;
> Pte. Norman LEE ;
> Pte. K. A. BRUCE ;
> Pte. R. J. BIDDLE ;
> Pte. O. A. SMART ;
> Pte. T. GIBSON ;

Pte. Ron CHESHAM ;
Pte. F. J. HULL ;
Gunner A. (George) IZZARD ;
Gunner O. GUNN ;
Pte. Ed. STANTON ;
Sapper E. C. WILLIAMS ;
Pte. James GOFF.[1]

Camden News, Thursday 1 August 1940, page 1.

SOLDIERS' FAREWELL

The second send-off to local volunteers who have enlisted for Active Service from the Camden District, attracted a record gathering on Friday night last. The function was arranged by the Camden Soldiers and Citizens' Association, and held in the Agricultural Hall, the attendance was calculated to be 900 persons. The President of the Association, Mr. W. S. Cruikshank, presided, and he had the assistance of his committee and other helpers.

The first portion of the evening was devoted to community singing, under the capable baton of Mr. H. C. Haylock, with Mr. H. V. Taplin as master of ceremonies. Mrs. H. S. Kelloway presided at the piano. Many patriotic and community songs were enjoyed and heartily entered into by the large assembly. Interspersed with these were items by Master Philip Haylock, Mrs. Norman Smith, Cpl. Colleen (R.A.A.F.), Mrs. Wilmington, Mr. Stan Richardson and Mr. S. G. Straney (magician).

Shortly after 9.30 p.m. the guests of the evening were assembled for a march on to the stage, and were led by local members of the old A.I.F. and welcomed by the chairman, Mr. Cruikshank, and the Mayor of Camden (Ald. H. S. Kelloway). The Mayor, with well chosen words, welcomed and congratulated the volunteers on behalf of the residents of the municipality, remarking that the wonderful gathering present that evening was evidence of the people's recognition of the loyal services their guests were offering to their country. On behalf of the district generally he wished them God speed and a safe return, and looked for the time when their welcome home will be enthusiastically greeted.

The presentation to each of the soldiers was made on behalf of the citizens by Wing Commander Bates, officer in command of the Central Flying School at Camden. He as senior serving officer said he did not wish to address the volunteers in the nature of a farewell, but rather he would welcome them into the Empire's service. Everybody realised the horror of bombing attacks and the devastation of the world by war, and no one wished to see it continued, but we do know and realise we will never lose our self-respect, and for that reason we will fight, and we will win. He knew the men had a big job in front of them, but they would have the comfort of knowing that all their hard work would be for the betterment of their country and Empire.

A pocket wallet, suitably inscribed, was then handed to each of the 29 guests. Mr. Cruikshank announcing the name as each volunteer stepped forward, and with a hearty handshake Wing Commander Bates congratulated each on his entry into the service.

The recipients were: —

Major E. Macarthur Onslow.
Aircraftsman A. Powell.
Gnr. J. N. Dunk.
Gnr. E. M. Rapley.
Gnr. Ben G. R. Sewell.
Gnr. C. K. Hain.
Gnr. Clifford W. Moffitt.
Gnr. A. Hoar.

Gnr. R. W. Crane.
Pte. J. R. Hoare.
Pte. R. J. Moffitt.
Pte. L. Suttle.
Pte. James R. Lee.
Pte. T. W. O'Brien.
Pte. A Hay.
Pte. T. J. Guyer.
Pte. H. S. Adams.
Pte. J. K. Dunbar.
Pte. E. H. McGrath.
Pte. J. C. Meredith.
Pte. W. J. Kelly.
Pte. E. J. Booth.
Pte. R. J. Auld.
Pte. Horace A. Gander.
Pte. D. A. Atfield.
Pte. J. Haynes.
Pte. Jack Menere.
Pte. L. Reed.
Signalman C. T. Adams.

A further presentation of a kit bag of useful articles was then made on behalf of the Women's Voluntary Services, to each of the soldiers, and prior to their departure from the stage, the audience rose and sang "For They are Jolly Good Fellows". Refreshments were provided by the Women's Voluntary Services, and the hall was cleared for dancing.

On Saturday night last the officers of Loyal Morning Star Lodge (MU. I.O.O.F.) made a presentation of a fountain pen to P.G. Bro. E. McGrath, who has enlisted in the A.I.F. The presentation was made by the N.G., P.G. Bro. Geo. Thorn, who wished Bro. McGrath the best of luck and a safe return to our shores.[2]

Camden News Thursday 24 October 1940, page 1

PUBLIC FAREWELL
To District Boys on Friday Night

The Soldiers & Citizens Association invite all to attend the third public farewell social to be held on Friday evening at the Agricultural Hall, Camden, in honour of the Camden and district residents who have enlisted in Australia's fighting forces.

A guard of honour will be formed by the men who saw service in the Great War of 1914-1918. Ex-service men are asked to be in attendance in the supper room at 8.30 p.m.

Proceedings will commence with community items at 8 o'clock. The presentations to the guests will take place at 9.30, who will later, with their immediate relatives, be entertained at supper. The Camden Centre of the Women's Voluntary Services, which has charge of the supper arrangements, will be pleased to receive donations of cakes, etc.

No public supper will be available on this occasion, owing to the almost impossible task of serving everyone in the hall.

Sergeant W. A. Evans is an addition to the list published in our last issue of those who are to be farewelled on Friday.[3]

Henry Jefferson Percival (Jeff) Bate

Lieutenant NX13862 (2139193)

Enlisted:	Australian Army, 20 May 1940 Paddington, NSW
Unit:	Australian Army Salvage Section
Born:	5 March 1906 Tilba Tilba, NSW
Parents:	Henry John Bate & Lily Percival
Occupation:	Farmer, Member of the Legislative Assembly
Spouse:	– Gerta Homburg; Married: 1928 Moruya, NSW
	– Thelma Kirby nee Olsen; Married: 12 June 1958, St Andrew's Presbyterian, Chatswood
	– Dame Zara Late Holt nee Dickins; Married: 19 February 1969 NSW
Residence:	Darlinghurst
Next of Kin:	Bate, Gerta
Died:	15 April 1984 Canberra, ACT
Buried:	Tilba Tilba General
Note:	Member for Wollondilly in 1938–1949. Member for Macarthur 1949–1972

Bate, Henry Jefferson Percival (Jeff)

Camden News Thursday 20 March 1941, page 6

LETTERS FROM SERGT. JEFF BATE, M.L.A.

30/l/'41 — We are still on our second ship and are lying anchored off a town in the East. Very soon now we will disembark. It has been a very good trip on this ship. The Sergeant's Quarters are excellent. To-day is gloriously cool, in fact the breeze coming over the desert is sweet and cold like Bowral in the spring. I have always thought of desert winds as blisteringly hot. We have been watching the city through glasses for a few days and can see cars, trains, ships, etc. The glasses have been marvellous; I am continually grateful for them. We have passed many mountains of tremendous height — absolutely barren and steep. Across the water now is one, about two or three thousand feet without any sign of a tree or a root or any living thing. I have not seen any water or streams. This morning we had our first real air raid and were able to put our drill into good use. It was about 4 a.m. and we saw the searchlights, heard gun and bomb blasts. The native boats and ships are picturesque. One big three-cornered sail pulled up to a long slanting pole. To-day has been very lovely. You can see many miles over the desert to more barren mountains, the colours of which are marvellous. The Egyptians and/or Arabs are very like the ones in the Anzac book. The nose in the drawing gives an idea of a Gyppo's and the fez is bright red with a darker tassel. The poor class people are dirty. Colour of Gyppos is much lighter than Indians on the ship. In fact they look like sunburned Italians slightly copper-coloured. It is rumoured that the sea mail is not much good, so will air mail this.

3/2/'41 — Have only just arrived and have been through Gaza at night and hope to see Jerusalem and Tel Aviv when I get leave. I like the district very much, being full of historic feeling from Abraham to Christ and from Saladin to the Jewish Revival — here also the old A.I.F. of 1914 war. Frost this morning, but a glorious warm day with cool breezes.

Have been quite busy with my bed of wickerwork which gently collapsed when I got on to it. I stayed down, and in the morning tied and braced and lashed it until it was strong enough. As I look down the hill now there is a camel train heavily laden, led by one 'wog' or Arab. "Enough" is leading a tired donkey. Usually a big Arab rides on the tail of a tired or badly fed donkey, although some of them are wonderfully strong little things. The two men are carrying heavy loads of sticks and hay on their heads while their lords supervise. The Arab is a marvellous thief, and as he has been disarmed I have to take extra ordinary precautions to guard my rifle. All fruits (oranges, grapefruit, limes — the best in the world form Jaffa) are disinfected in Condy's crystals for half an hour before use. You must not put your naked or stockinged feet on the ground for fear of hookworms. Such a lot of things like that to learn. Will write about agriculture I saw in Egypt as I came through. I saw a battleship on the sand moving along, but later found it to be on the Suez Canal.

4/2/'41 — I am thrilled to feel I am in Palestine because ever since I could hear and see I have been trained to know about Gaza and the Philistines and Jerusalem and David and Christ and Bethlehem. Contrary to pictures of the sand and hills, this country is remarkably fertile, and so far the climate is superb. We seem to hold an even temperature from about 10 a.m. Before that the mornings are cold and fresh but afterwards the sun is just warm with a fragrant sweet breeze just moving all day. Probably the gentle influence of the Mediterranean, five miles away, gives us a good climate. It is like Tilba in the winter. The orange orchard has the healthiest young trees with huge, lush leaves, dark green, massed with huge colourful fruit of rather over-juicy quality. This may have been caused by recent rains.

Both in Egypt and Palestine the farmer or peasant is very poor and dirty. Apparently it never rains in the section of Egypt I saw, because the houses of peasants were mud walls with a few pieces of brushwood over the top for shade. The water for plants and drinking, etc. must all come from the Nile in canals which are also used for barges propelled by sails. Everywhere in Egypt and Palestine are donkeys and camels and more of the zebu strain of cattle. Cattle, camels and donkeys are used for raising water from wells where the Nile cannot reach. They are trained to walk round in a circle unattended while the water pours from the primitive machine. The Arab villages are of mud walls, mud houses with earth roof on which oats or barley grows. Perfect camouflage, apparently quite unintentional. They are indescribably filthy, and the children have suppurating eyes. The yards inside mud walls smell frightfully. The old Biblical head-dress survives and seems to be two elastic black girdles on the head to keep the contraption in place. The Arabs ride donkeys everywhere. Large dirty Arabs on tiny donkeys. They sit tight on the hind quarters. Camel trains go through and give their riders an atrocious seat. The plough teams are sometimes 1 heifer, 1 camel and 1 donkey, but the cultivation is painstakingly good. No trees anywhere, not even palms, and in rich friable country there is bad erosion. Australians have planted thousands of gumtrees, which are doing well and give you a thrill of home. Palestine and Australia seem to be very closely together.[4]

Camden News Thursday 10 July 1941, page 7

SERGT. JEFF BATE, M.L.A.
FROM THE MIDDLE EAST

Notes from letters received by Mrs. Bate from her husband, Sergt. Jeff Bate, M.L.A., on active service.

We have moved from our desert camp, though there is plenty of sand here, and this place has many of the advantages of a week-end camp (swimming, sunbaking). We beg coal from passing trains and had some success to-night when a single locomotive pulled up and we traded our bully beef for some. The driver came down to the galley and got a double handful of tea leaves. While this went on one of our more enterprising fellows hopped up on the tender and got about 2 cwt., not as good as our Aussie coal. When the Gyppo soldiers told us they get 30/- per month and corporals £4 per month with £1 allowance for food, you realise that a few tins of bully mean a lot to these wogs.

Guma, who is a Sudanese, has ignored all our efforts to chase him from our camp, and is now installed as "Gunga Dhin" and is the most useful fellow here. He just burnt his thumb and we used the Tannafax. The First Aid kit has been most useful.

Your cablegram and letters of the 9th and 11th April arrived together. Naturally I was very thrilled to be unopposed, and felt it was a tribute to the A.I.F. and a sign that people at home still have the high principles of the last war. They recognise that service is a matter of duty and of first importance. It is a horrible business but must be done. Please thank all those in Wollondilly who have been good enough to think so kindly of us that they returned me unopposed.

Do not be disturbed over my letter saying I may not be able to write from our new spot. The opportunities to do so are unrivalled and it appears very peaceful and beautiful.

I am sleeping under some low trees like our Sally wattle on a bed of leaves. First one puts down a rubber waterproof groundsheet, then a doubled thick camel hair and wool blanket (I think they are British service issue) then one crawls into a doubled soft grey woolly Australian blanket, with another single one tucked over the top.

I am loving the outdoor life and will never demur at camping when I get back. There always seems to be a thrill in starting in a new place.

I don't think I have ever mentioned the Egyptian marrows. These are small, like a lot of their produce, but in this case it makes them more tasty. In Eastern Mediterranean countries there are plenty of tomatoes and cucumbers, and a very sweet lettuce with straight leaves and no heart.

You would wonder how the Mediterranean ever has a tempest with its calm purple-blue water. There is usually not even the slightest swell, and on the beaches are a few ripples. I have been swimming and sunbaking on a rocky coast, where you can dive into the clearest water I have ever seen. It is very salty and this may cause less algal growth than on our coast. You can open your eyes down below and distinguish other people.

There are many eucalyptus here and we appreciate them.

Tomorrow will be a year since that terrible day when I went into camp and you went into hospital. It has been a very eventful year with enough changes and movement to satisfy me.

When you mention relief at getting a cable I realise that you must have worried because you don't know what is happening until days afterwards. As a matter of fact, I think we are doing absolutely nothing, like the five bob a day tourists that we read about in some March papers. Some day we hope we will get some action.

Up to the present Australians have fought with marvellous bravery, and deserve all that apparently overdone publicity. When you see conditions in other parts of the world — poverty, overcrowding, malnutrition — then our magnificent well-fed, sunburnt lads are just head and shoulders above all others, including English and Germans. I do not include English Armoured Troops, because they are superb. Ordinary English Infantry say that if the Australians had been allowed to stay in Greece they would have made it terribly awkward for the Germans, even without any aeroplanes at all. I really believe the in habitants of this place look on the Aussies as sort of gods and regard them as real fighters who never know when they are beaten. Perhaps I have changed, as in previous letters I praised British personnel. Since then I have heard eye witnesses' stories of the real thing and it makes me proud to be an Australian.

There is too much hysteria in Australia about the war. People's judgment would be better if they examined matters more calmly.

Please convey to all kind friends my heartfelt gratitude and relief at the result of nominations for Wollondilly. Tell them I hope that Germany will soon collapse from inside so that I can return to work with them once more.

In sleeping on the ground I always make a hip and shoulder hole. If I forget and move I have a very bad sleep. Blackouts with blued street lights are the usual thing over here, and one gets quite used to it. Taxis become essential, and they are frightening, swinging about with very dimmed lights.

Our mail is much less regular now, and to-day's, the first for a fortnight, brought your parcel, letters and a bundle of papers. I was disappointed there was no mail from the children but the parcel made up for everything. Except for some lanoline on the stockings, it was undamaged and was very well chosen. I can't get chewing gum over here, it saves me drinking too much water on hot days.

This morning I went to the first Church Parade for months. The Padre was from an English unit. He had the usual detached style of English officers, so different from direct Australian ways, but made up for it by speaking very briefly. He said we should not pray to be safe, but to be used, that God might use our eyes, brains, hands, etc. A large number of men attended Communion and it was a great help.

Like all other places where there are Imperial troops, the wives of English troops and officers are either evacuated or are expected to help at canteens. As a result there is a good Garrison Club where we get some good cheap food on leave. They have a fruit salad made of mixed stewed fruit, to which I add ice cream and enjoy very much. There is a radio on which we get some very skimpy Australian news, broadcast by Jerusalem.

The rooms of the Club, which was a large two storey mansion, are very good, and I like the illustrated papers and copies of "The Times". All our actions are spoken of as British Troops, or Imperial Troops, but never as Australian, so apparently many British people get only a one-eyed view of our exertions here, but the Middle East people have no illusions.

One of the songs the lads sing is "And when the war is over and everything is swell, Our girls will go with the boys they know and we can go to Hell."

From this distance the old stuff in Aussie papers is very narrow. What a gorgeous country it is and how fortunate are its people! Even the lowest paid relief worker is better off than well paid workers here.

The population here is mainly Greek and very friendly to Australians. Last night a doctor, a news editor, a school teacher, a chemist, and a journalist befriended me in a restaurant, fed me generously and took me to the cinema, where they gave me coffee, lemonade and cigarettes.

Unfortunately 99 per cent. of the farms are so small that they cannot run stock for milk like we do. They milk sheep, goats or yoked bovine stock. Milk is not sold as in Sydney. There are no milk bars, but brandy and wine are 1/- and less per bottle. Natives drink spirits like we drink beer or cordials by the large glass.

Young Greeks come into the camp and for a shave and haircut I paid 5 piastres, which works out cheaper than one Valet blade. I am getting on well with the Greek language[5].

James Clark DFC, AFC

Squadron Leader 402439

Enlisted:	Royal Australian Air Force 19 August 1940 Sydney, NSW
Unit:	460 Squadron
Born:	28 August 1915 Waverley, NSW
Parents:	David Clark & Mary M Kilpatrick
Occupation:	Assistant Secretary Camden Park Estate
Spouse:	Ivy Eileen
Residence:	Hurstville, NSW
Next of Kin:	David Clark
Died:	Killed in Action over Germany 12th December 1944
Buried:	Reichswald Forest War Cemetery, Kleve, Nordrhein-Westfalen, Germany 13.G.12
Honours:	Honours Distinguished Flying Cross, Air Force Cross
Roll of Honour:	Camden, NSW

Clark, James

Camden News Thursday 1 November 1945, page 4

Mr. D. Clark, of 18 John Street, Hurstville, has received the following message from the Department of Air: — "All efforts to trace your son, Squadron Leader James Clark, D.F.C., A.C.F., have proved unavailing, and it is feared that all hope of finding him alive must be abandoned."[6]

James Clark (sitting)

Rupert Frederick Arding (Derick) Downes

Sergeant Pilot 402660

Enlisted:	Royal Australian Air Force 18 September 1940 Sydney.
Unit:	1 (Middle East) Training School
Born:	28 August 1919, Camden, NSW
Parents:	Rupert Frederick Arding Downes & Katie May Elizabeth Coghill Maddrell
Occupation:	Grazier
Married:	19 February 1969 St Andrew's Presbyterian, Chatswood NSW
Residence:	'Aston' Brownlow Hill, Camden, NSW
Next of Kin:	R Downes
Discharged:	7 October 1942
Died:	Killed on Service Middle East 7 October 1942
Buried:	Moascar War Cemetery, Egypt. 4.B.15
Memorial:	Memorial light St. Paul's C/E Cobbitty
Roll of Honour:	Camden, NSW
Note:	Killed in aircraft accident involving Hurricane I Z.4031

Downes, Rupert Frederick Arding (Derick)

Camden News Thursday 15 October 1942, page 4

SGT. PILOT R. F. A. DOWNES KILLED

Camden mourns the sad loss of another member of the fighting forces. Sergt. Pilot (Derick) Downes, who fell at his country's service on 7th October.

Derick, the only son of Mr. and Mrs. R. F. A. Downes, of "Aston", Brownlow Hill, enlisted with the R.A.A.F. in 1940, at the age of 21 years, and after preliminary training was transferred to Southern Rhodesia, where he received his wings and promoted Sergt. Pilot. For two years he has been on Active Service, and it was only on Saturday last his parents received word from the Air Board stating that it had been reported their son had lost his life in an aircraft accident on the 7th October. The accident happened presumably in the Middle East.

The deepest sympathy of the community goes out to the bereaved parents and sisters.[7]

John Hurst Edmondson VC

Corporal NX15705

Enlisted:	Australian Army, 20 May 1940 Paddington, NSW
Unit:	2/17 Australian Infantry Battalion
Born:	8 October 1914 Wagga Wagga, NSW
Parents:	Joseph William Edmondson & Maude Elizabeth Hurst
Occupation:	Farmer
Residence:	Liverpool, NSW
Next of Kin:	Joseph Edmondson
Died:	Killed in Action Tobruk, Lybia 14 April 1941
Buried:	Tobruk War Cemetery, Tobruk, Libya
Honours:	Victoria Cross
Roll of Honour:	Liverpool, NSW
Note:	Council member of the Liverpool Agricultural Society and acted as a steward at its shows.

Edmondson, John Hurst

Adem Road near Post R33. This strong-point was garrisoned by the 2nd/17th's No.16 Platoon in which Edmondson was a section leader. The enemy intended to clear the post as a bridgehead for an armoured assault on Tobruk.

Under cover of darkness thirty Germans infiltrated the barbed wire defences, bringing machine-guns, mortars and two light field-guns. Lieutenant Austin Mackell, commanding No.16 Platoon, led Edmondson's five-man section in an attempt to repel the intruders. Armed with rifles, fixed bayonets and grenades, the party of seven tried to outflank the Germans, but were spotted by the enemy who turned their machine guns on them. Unknown to his mates, Edmondson was severely wounded in the neck and stomach. Covering fire from R33 ceased at the pre-arranged time of 11.45 p.m. and Mackell ordered his men to charge.

John Edmondson

Despite his wounds, Edmondson accounted for several enemy soldiers and saved Mackell's life. When the remaining Germans fled, the Australians returned to their lines. Although Edmondson was treated for his wounds, he died before dawn on 14 April 1941. The Germans' armoured attack that morning was thwarted, partly due to the earlier disruption of their plans. Edmondson was buried in Tobruk war cemetery. He had not married.

His Victoria Cross gazetted on 4 July, was the first awarded to a member of Australia's armed forces in World War II.

Camden News Thursday 2 October 1941, page 1

PUBLIC MEETING
THE LATE CORPORAL JOHN HURST EDMONDSON, V.C.

Corporal Edmondson VC

The public meeting held at the Council Chambers, Bringelly, was attended by the Deputy President of the Nepean Shire (Cr. W. Rose) and Crs. Rudd, Scott, and Watson, together with over twenty residents of the shire.

The chairman drew attention to the decision of the council to call this meeting of residents for the purpose of discussing ways and means of suitably commemorating the late Corporal John Edmondson, V.C. services to Australia, and mentioned that this young man had lived practically all his life in the Nepean Shire. He was of a well respected family, his father had given service to the people as a Councillor of the Shire, and that the council had felt that a memorial to this young man within the Shire would be very fitting, and mentioned that several suggestions had been made in regard to the form the proposed memorial should take. The following had been brought under his notice: — A plaque in the Council Chambers, a home for a war widow, a scholarship, a monument, the purchase of War Bonds for the erection of a memorial to be decided at the end of the war.

The chairman at this stage formally introduced Mr. Shaw, the recently appointed shire clerk, who had consented to assist in this meeting.

Cr. Rose read a number of apologies, and said he had been assured by many others who were unable to be present that they would be behind the project. He suggested that the meeting be quite free in its discussions, and perhaps first of all decide on the establishment of a fund.

Mr. Young moved that residents of the Nepean Shire establish a memorial to the late Cpl. Edmondson, V.C, within the Nepean Shire, in a form to be decided upon later, and those present constitute a committee therefore with power to add to their numbers, to further the project. Mr. Anderson seconded. Carried.

Cr. T. G. Scott said he was very pleased to see such a goodly number of people present, and so representative, in view of the difficulties, and suggested that those present might give consideration to the provision of a monument to be erected at the corner of the Hume Highway and Bringelly Rd. close to the home that our departed friend left to do his duty, to be in the form of a fountain, a water trough and dog trough. He mentioned the water and dog troughs as Mr. Edmondson had informed him that his son was particularly fond of animals and would have liked this suggestion.

Mr. Paterson suggested that whilst he was prepared to fall in with the majority, his ideas would naturally lie in the selection of a memorial to take the form of a scholarship or bursary. He was supported in this matter by Mr. Young and others.

Further discussion ensued, and Cr. Scott said that to test the feeling of the meeting, he would place his proposal in the form of a motion, and moved, seconded by Mr. Wheatley, that a fountain be erected with water trough and dog trough as a memorial to the late Cpl. Edmondson, V.C. , at the corner of the Hume Highway and Bringelly Rd., and provision be made thereon for the names of each enlistee of the shire, and those referred to who failed to return.

The motion was fully discussed and attention was drawn to the fact that if the motion was carried, it would be necessary to obtain the approval of the Nepean Shire, the Main Roads Dept. and maybe others. Cr. Rose promised that he would approach the necessary authorities in this regard. It was definitely agreed that if this motion was carried the memorial would be known as "The Edmondson Memorial," although other names would be placed thereon as it was felt that the late Cpl. Edmondson would like the names of the other enlistees of the Shire associated with this memorial.

The motion was put to the meeting and carried.

Moved by Messrs. Shaw and Clink that a general committee be elected, comprising a chairman, who shall be the President of the Nepean Shire Council; vice presidents, who shall be all the other Councillors of the Shire; and other persons elected: the secretary and treasurer. This was put to the meeting and carried.

Moved by Mr. Wheatley, seconded by Cr. Scott, that Mr. Shaw be appointed secretary and Mr. Paterson, treasurer. Carried. Moved by Messrs. Paterson and Downes that in addition to the councillors and vice presidents, Messrs. Young, Anderson, Clink and Wheatley be elected vice presidents. Carried. Moved by Messrs. Paterson and Story that the fund be inaugurated and lists be opened for donations. Carried.

The meeting decided on the motion of Messrs. Young and Downes that the Nepean Shire Council be requested to obtain designs and prices of suitable memorials.

Moved by Messrs. Paterson and Clink that lists remain open until the end of October, and that the next general meeting be held at the Council Chambers, on Thursday November 13th.

Subscriptions may be left at either the offices of The Camden News or Campbelltown News.

In closing the meeting the Chairman thanked all for their attendance.[8]

James Healy

Private NX68937 (23157)

Enlisted:	Australian Army 5 March 1941 Paddington, NSW
Unit:	2/3 Australian Infantry Battalion
Born:	19 January 1921 Doncaster, England
Residence:	Narellan, NSW
Next of Kin:	Malony
Discharged:	19 February 1946
Died:	25 September 1997 Woy Woy, NSW

Healy, James

In the Second World War Pte James (Jim) Healy fought in the Middle East and in New Guinea with the 2/3rd battalion.

War Memorial records state that the 2/3rd Battalion was raised at Victoria Barracks, Sydney on 24 October 1939. It relocated to the newly-opened Ingleburn Camp on 2 November. On 10 January 1940, it sailed from Sydney and disembarked in Egypt on 14 February. After further training in Palestine and Egypt, the 2/3rd took part in its first campaign - the advance against the Italians in eastern Libya - in January 1941. It was involved in the successful attacks at Bardia and Tobruk, and remained as part of the Tobruk garrison when the advance continued. The 2/3rd left Tobruk on 7 March, ultimately bound, with the rest of the 6th Division, for Greece.

Arriving in Greece on 19 March, the 2/3rd was deployed north to resist the German invasion. The 2/3rd supported the 2/2nd Battalion and blocked German movement through the gorge, allowing the unhindered withdrawal of Allied forces further south. Activities in Greece ended with evacuation by sea from Kalamata on 27 April.

In June and July 1941, the 2/3rd took part in the campaign in Syria and Lebanon and fought around Damascus. The battalion left the Middle East, heading for the war against Japan, on 10 March 1942.

The 2/3rd's first campaign against the Japanese was the advance along the Kokoda Trail to the Japanese beachheads between September and December 1942. The 2/3rd's last campaign of the war was the operation to clear the Japanese from the Wewak region of New Guinea between December 1944 and August 1945. The 2/3rd Battalion disbanded on 8 February 1946.

Healy later joined a Port Operating Company and became a salvage diver.

Michel Eugene (Mike) Kartzoff

Warrant Officer Class 2 NX16460

Enlisted:	Australian Army, 22 May 1940 Paddington, NSW
Unit:	Liverpool Prisoner of War & Internment Camp
Born:	27 February 1908 Kiev, Russia
Married:	Rona Margaret
Next of Kin:	E Wittigeustein
Discharged:	26 September 1945
Died:	29 December 1987
Buried:	Macquarie Park Lawn Cemetery
Note:	Divorced 1960

Kartzoff, Michel Eugene (Mike)

Camden News Thursday 5 August 1943, page 3

SERGT. MICHEL KARTZOFF
SOLDIERS' INDEPENDENT CANDIDATE

Sergt. Michel Kartzoff who has come from a Northern battle station to contest the Werriwa seat as an Independent Service candidate, is well known in the Campbelltown and Camden districts, having been a member of the 1st Light Horse before the war, and having enlisted in 1940 in an A.I.F. Machine Gun Battalion, in which are serving a number of the local lads. Sergt. Kartzoff only returned from the Middle East 5 months ago with the Ninth Division. He said that the members of the A.I.F. had been bitterly disappointed to find on their return home that the country had sunk into a state of bureaucratic chaos with a widespread indifference to the war effort, short of commodities, unwarranted strikes and profiteering. It was then that he decided to stand for Parliament.

Looking deeper into matters, said Mr. Kartzoff, I perceived that these things were not the root of the evil but symptoms of a much more serious disease. Take for instance the soaring prices and the shortage of food stuffs. We are told that it is due to the shortage of manpower. I say there is no shortage of manpower. What about the thousands of soldiers unfit for front line service, and for whom there are no base jobs, and yet who are unable to obtain a discharge? What about the shockingly over staffed cost-plus jobs and the wastage of manpower in the C.C.C. due to maladministration? What about the manpower wasted through strikes, and the preposterous number of people employed in enforcing various regulations? Meanwhile rural districts are overrun with pests and many farms have only men and women left.–M. Kartzoff, Broughton St. Campbelltown.[9]

Camden News Thursday 12 August 1943, page 4

WERRIWA CANDIDATE
SERGT. KARTZOFF

On the only Russian candidate:–

Hubert Peter Lazzarini, Minister for Home Security, has attracted the opposition of Michel Kartzoff, the one and only Russian candidate. Michel is of the same breed as Shaposhnikov, Stalin's Chief of the General Staff, born at Kiev in the Ukraine of an old military family. He speaks half a dozen languages. He saw the Germans occupy the Ukraine, in the last war, saw the civil war through, then emigrated to what seemed the quieter realm of Italy, but had barely matriculated in Naples University when the Fascist revolution exploded.

Wisely, he decided to get as far from erupting Europe as possible, and for 17 years or so he has been farm worker, builders' assistant, gold miner, Matilda waltzer, journalist and exponent of half a dozen other erudite trades, filling in his time with voracious reading on foreign affairs and social sciences. Four years before the war he became an ardent volunteer member of the Light Horse and, enlisting for overseas service early in 1940, went off with the crack A.I.F. machine gun unit to Palestine, the Western Desert and Syria. He was at Alamein with the 8th Army. His last journey was a 1200 miles hitchhike from a northern battle station to get at Comrade Lazzarini who represents an electorate which gave the Ninth Division a lot of its hardiest members, including Sergeant Kartkoff's Coy. — "The Bulletin."

Between June 1940, and May 1943, 2,400,000 tons of Axis shipping were sunk in the Mediterranean. Of this more than 1,000,000 tons were sunk by submarines.[10]

Lewis (Lew) Charles Marriott

Flight Lieutenant 404802 (O16105)

Enlisted:	Royal Australian Air Force, 8 November 1940 Brisbane, Qld
Unit:	RAAF Station Laverton
Born:	4 April 1922 Brisbane, Qld
Parents:	Vincent Frederick Marriott & Lillian Alice
Married:	Marion
Residence:	Grange, Qld
Next of Kin:	Vivian Marriott
Discharged:	17 January 1946
Died:	8 May 2008 Carrington Nursing Home, Camden, NSW
Note:	Living in Springfield Road, Catherine Field

Marriott, Lewis (Lew) Charles

**At Sea,
12 January 1941**

Dear Mum, Dad, etc.

On our way again. Suva was a quaint place with so many natives about the place. You most likely have my card from Fiji but we were rather unfortunate as we were only allowed 6 hours leave and this being from 6 p.m. to 12 p.m. However the boat didn't sail till about 2 p.m. the next day and so we had rather a good look from the ship which commanded an excellent view of Suva. The native Fijians very dark indeed, in fact even blacker than the Abos I have seen, and an amazing feature is the pink hands these chaps have.

I took quite a few snaps of the island which are really very scenic. In fact all told so far I have taken about 80 snaps. The

Lewis Marriott

Fijian is not only very polite but very smart. The police force consisting practically entirely of natives is very efficient. The native dress is rather amazing as the men wear skirts but you'll see all this when I eventually bring my snaps home.

Since leaving Suva the ocean has still been calm although occasionally there is a slight swell. At present we are well and truly in the tropics and oh boy is it hot. Of a night time we only wear our pyjama pants to sleep in and during the day it is compulsory for us to stay on deck as much as possible. There is a swimming pool rigged up on the aft deck and so we swim quite a bit. The work is starting again and although today is Sunday we have our time occupied till 5.30 tonight. The ship passed over the International Date Line and so we had an extra day this week. Come to think of it, we went to bed on Friday night and woke up on Friday morning. I think the Equator is crossed at 7 a.m. tomorrow morning and I believe there is to be the usual King Neptune visit.

13 January 1941

As I said the Equator was crossed this morning and King Neptune certainly went to work.

I don't think I have ever had such a ducking in all my life. The Neptune police just simply marched up and took us one by one and after covering our face with flour and water and then shaving us with a large wooden razor they just simply tossed us clothes and all into the swimming pool. It is still very hot and I think I have sun baked for about 3 hours all told and I have never been so black.

14 January 1941

For the first time the ship is starting to roll and it is good. But alas I have just had a big luncheon and so here's hoping. At the table one of my unreliable friends had the nerve to bet me 5 cents that I would be sick first and did I take him on. I should say so. I don't think I have ever felt better. Yesterday I went on parade with a button undone and so today I have to do 6 hours watch; nice chaps our officers!

But it isn't as bad as it seems as today they gave us about 20 cigarettes each. Thank heaven too, for I believe we don't get paid for about 3 weeks after we arrive in Canada and I'm very nearly broke now – still that's just too bad.

15 January 1941

Now to resume. It appears as though we are in luck as after I had finished writing yesterday we were called together and each man was issued with a Certificate from Neptune. The certificate is enclosed. We were told also that although we are not allowed ashore at Honolulu the natives are turning on a show for us on the wharf which will result in each airman receiving some American Comforts. I don't think I have mentioned before that we have also received quite a few supplies since being on the ship from the Aust. Comforts Fund.

On parade this morning we were told the astonishing fact that the RAAF was giving a show, for the benefit of officers and ship's company. To make matters worse I have to take part in it, still I'll tell you all about it later.

I suppose by now all the festive spirit has relaxed and school has started once more. Oh that reminds me. Ray, how are the Rovers going? If at all. You might let us know all about it, and will you give Maurie my Canadian address please.

Well I'm afraid if this letter has to catch the mail from Honolulu I shall have to close and so trusting you are all enjoying the best health.

Your loving son

Lewis

P.S. I'll send an air mail letter as soon as I get paid.

Cranwell, Sleaford, England
1 October 1941

Dear Mum, Dad & all at home

Another week gone by so to write once again and as before you will note that I have again been posted. This time to the RAF Station at Cranwell, near Sleaford in the county of Lincolnshire. We left Bournemouth on Monday morning and after travelling all day we arrived there in the late evening so we saw a good deal of England on the way. As before everybody was very impressed, the countryside being very green and beautiful. One of the stations through which we passed was Oxford and the famous varsity was visible.

In most of the larger towns the damage caused by air raids is unmistakable. However there is quite a lot of England still untouched and nowadays the people don't even bother about going into shelters. We have been issued with anti-gas equipment and steel helmets which we have to carry at all times.

The station here at Cranwell is the permanent RAF Base in peace time so it is gigantic. The only trouble is that I am not allowed to tell you just what I am doing but I should not be on operation for a couple of months yet. The provisions made for sport are excellent so I am looking forward to tennis, golf, football and swimming. All told I believe there are 12 courts and the swimming is performed in a heated indoor pool. I have arranged to play tennis this afternoon so I will let you know all about it in my next. For evening amusement there is a proper picture house on the station which shows nightly, and dancing is conducted on two evenings a week. Also stationed in the near vicinity to our particular wing are 1,500 WAAF so we won't be stuck for company. As a matter of fact last night while dancing I met a very pretty WAAF who I am hoping to see a lot of.

I am afraid that once again I must do some more appealing as on this station they don't even use the words chocolate or sweets and we are allowed to buy 60 cigarettes per fortnight. In fact any tinned stuff no matter what it be would certainly be appreciated.

Well that seems to be all for this week but when we settle down I should be able to get more news. As for the weather, it is fairly cold although we usually have sunshine. I think most of us are a little worried as to what it is going to be like in winter so we are keeping our fingers crossed. Now I shall have to close so trusting you are all well and hoping to get some mail in the near future.

Your loving son
Lewis
PS - This is the third air mail letter I have posted since my arrival in England.
Lewis

RAAF,
Thornaby
6 February 1942

Dear Mum, Dad & all at home,
To open I had better mention our change of address before I forget:
Aust 404802 Sgt Marriott L.C.

c/- Overseas Headquarters,
Royal Australian Air Force
Kodak House
Kingsway
LONDON WC2

This seems to be an improvement as I have received two more air mail letters, 4 parcels and 3 newspapers. The parcels were from Auntie Phoebe, Auntie Emily, yours and 1 from the McWhirters. The contents came in very handy and are being enjoyed to the full by my friends and myself. According to your letter Mr. Bingham has left so I will miss him. However I will make enquiries as soon as I get leave. I heard from Mrs. Cross recently but the letter was written before X'mas so I do not know if the parcel has arrived. Please let Mrs. Lowry know I was very sorry to read about Toby but he is bound to turn up. That my letters are hitting the radio was certainly a surprise. The only thing left to do with them is to write a book when it is all over.

Now for the great news. Since last writing I have had four hours dual instruction in the air. Oh Boy! does it feel great to be at the controls. I was climbing, gliding, diving, banking, steep turning, slipping, etc. and I have even done a landing. Now I am trying very hard for a remustering but I don't think my dreams will be realised until I have completed my operational hours. The midway examinations have been terminated with myself topping three subjects and coming second in a fourth. We have had a couple of flights with our operational crates and they are very efficient and comfortable. My only hope is that me able to fly it out to the Far East front, enabling me to have a much desired crack against those cheeky little yellow "B's". As per usual we are having a snow fall on every odd day which is resulting in occasional fights with snowballs. Although we would all prefer the warmer weather of home we are making the best of what we can get. We have had another couple of crew parties and I have seen a couple of rather oldish pictures. Well that seems to be all for now so I will close to resume next week.

Trusting you are all well and hoping to be with you all in the near future.

Your loving son and brother,
Lewis

RAAF England
30 December 1942

Dear Mum, Dad and All at home,

Once again the Xmas celebrations are over. As was expected we did not get the opportunity of a few days leave. I expect you have all had a marvellous time at Margate[i].

On the 23rd I received two of your letters together with a letter from Heather. Actually I could not have wished for a better present.

The entertainment started last Wednesday when we went to the Glenmount Theatre in Chichester and saw "Coastal Command"[ii]. It was quite a change to sit and watch somebody else doing the work. I recommend that you see the film and so get an idea of what our part is in this war. The Australian W/AG[iii] in the Hudson was trained with me and he was also in the same squadron until he was killed in action on the same kind of work he portrayed in the film.[iv]

Xmas eve for us was rather disappointing as we were detailed for flying. Naturally this stopped any entertainment. The entertaining our officers in our mess started Xmas day with a wow. The dinner was gigantic. Turkey was the main item together with the usual pudding. As usual the pudding did not interest me but the turkey etc. went down very well. A dance in the Airmen's Dining Hall ended the day well. Boxing Day saw us in the Officers Mess as their guests. There is no doubt about it they do certainly have the best of everything. In the evening a few of us saw "Robin Hood" in Havant.[v]

Living up to the usual Xmas tradition the station got up a pantomime which was presented on Sunday evening in the station cinema. Although rather amateurish the presentation, "Cinderella" was very entertaining.

Monday and last night were both party nights. First we had our squadron's effort. This was an all- men affair and between consuming mugs of beer the chaps put on some clever sketches. As can be expected dirty stories ruled supreme. Last night was the WAAF night and their party took the form of a dance with refreshment.

I am ever so pleased that the garden party was such a success and that more mail has arrived. Fancy Heather winning the shopping bag! I think you must have worked it. The malaria seems to be giving Dave a tough spell. So tomorrow is the last day of this year. I wonder what 1943 has in store for us. Trusting you are all enjoying the very best of health.

Love to all,
Your loving son Lewis

---

[i] Margate, Qld.
[ii] 1943 British film made by the Crown Film Unit for the Ministry of Information. The film, distributed by RKO, dramatized the work of RAF Coastal Command. The film starred Pilot Roger Hunter (as himself) Flight Sergeant Charles Norman Lewis (also as himself).
[iii] Wireless Air Gunner
[iv] Sergeant Richard Wyke Allop, 402455 1 Coastal Operational Training RAF was killed in an aircraft accident 28 December 1941 Cumberland, England
[v] A town in Hampshire

AUS404802 P/O Marriott L.C., RAAF Base PO
Kingsway, London
10 June 1943

Dear Mum, Dad and all at home,

Your congratulatory cable and letter and a parcel have arrived since I last took up my pen. Thanks a million the parcel was a beaut. Unfortunately the parcel containing the clothing must have been lost. However now that I have clothing coupons I have restocked in every department. I wish you could see me in all my regalia.[i]

There is no doubt about it, the malaria seems to be knocking the troops about, I hope both Freddie Rae and Dere get over it ok. The rest must have been an enjoyable change for Ray. You must be very busy. Strange you should mention tennis for only this week I had a knock over. Naturally the form isn't the best but I hope to pick up again. The trouble is the balls which are practically unprocurable. Being an officer has opened up new opportunities for me to play squash. I like this game very much and most officers' messes have courts. I have had a couple of hard games this week.

Since last writing I have completed another operational sortie. On our weekly day off we went into town again and you can imagine our surprise when we were able to get steak and mushrooms. I still am not allowed to give you any details. After this meal we went to a dance but the last bus back to camp is 10 o'clock so we didn't get in much dancing.

This censorship is a curse as apart from not being able to mention work and weather I cannot tell you where I am. Because of this I am afraid this must be a short letter. I trust you are all enjoying the same good health as I am.

Love to all,

Your loving son Lewis.

---

[i] Marriott was appointed "Pilot Officer" effective 27/02/1943

Gordon John McLeod

Warrant Officer 42144

Enlisted:	Royal Australia Air Force 1 February 1942 Sydney, NSW
Unit:	299 Squadron
Born:	2 March 1922 Armidale, NSW
Parents:	Douglas John McLeod & Una Gertrude Vickers
Spouse:	Ina Jean Rideout; Married: 1 December 1951 St. John's C/E Camden, NSW
Next of Kin:	Douglas McLeod
Discharged:	13 September 1945

McLeod, Gordon John

The Camden Museum has two items donated by Gordon McLeod. One is a rectangular, very thin coloured silk map of "Zones of France W.E.A. March 1944", showing occupied areas in World War Two. 62 x 57 cm. It was issued to Gordon McLeod during World War Two as part of his air force survival kit as Warrant Officer/Gunner on a Stirling Bomber in Squadron 149.

Gordon also donated to the Camden Museum a framed colour photo of a painting by T. Marchant of a Stirling bomber on a bombing raid over Berlin in World War Two. Gordon was present at the bombing of Berlin on 22nd November 1943. He actually flew in this Stirling Mark 3 bomber L- OJ on bombing raids to Germany. He was the Mid-Upper Gunner (MUG) on the plane in the painting. He was in Squadron 149 (East India).

In the 1970s Gordon McLeod was the auditor of the Camden Historical Society.

Warrant Officer McLeod

William (Bill) Mundell

Sergeant NX9275

Enlisted:	Australian Army, 21 December 1939, Paddington, NSW
Unit:	2/1 Field Company
Born:	11 October 1917 Dalbeattie, Scotland
Parents:	Samuel Cairns Mundell & Florence Edgar
Occupation:	Assistant Mechanic
Spouse:	Sarah Scholes; Married: 1945 Camden, NSW
Residence:	Orangeville, NSW
Next of Kin:	Samual Cairns (father)
Discharged:	22 October 1945

Mundell, William (Bill)

Camden News Thursday 4 January 1940, page 1

WEROMBI NEWS
FAREWELL TO Pte. W. MUNDELL

Werombi's first Digger of the 2nd A.I.F., in the person of Pte. Wm. Mundell, was tendered a farewell and presentation in the local Parish Hall last Saturday night. As this gathering is the first of its kind during the present war, it was pleasing to see the large assembly of friends to pay homage to a very popular young man, who is expecting to sail with the first of our troops. Local Diggers of the old A.I.F. were in strong support. Digger Norman Mackie, acting as M.C., kept the evening's proceedings well in hand. The guest of the evening on arrival was escorted by the Misses Joan Morris and Elaine Clowes through a guard of honour (formed up by local members of the old A.I.F.) to the centre of the hall to the accompaniment of, "He's a jolly good fellow," followed by the National Anthem. Dancing followed until about 10

William Mundell

p.m., when Digger O. Morris was called upon to make a presentation on behalf of the residents of Werombi and Orangeville to Pte. W. Mundell. Eulogistic references were made to Bill's sterling qualities, who had for the last twelve years made his home with Mrs. M. Stewart and the late J. B. Stewart, whose influences helped to mould a very fine character. On handing Pte. Mundell a splendid fountain pen and ever-sharp pencil, the presenter wished him good luck and a speedy return. Digger J. Clowes, in support, hoped they would finish this war and not leave it half-done like the last one. He also wished him God speed and a safe return.

Pte. Mundell, after much handclapping, suitably responded. The ladies in the meantime had not been idle, and on supper being served they had the tables beautifully decorated and laden with tasty eatables, which were much enjoyed and appreciated by all.

A late comer to the evening was Pte. Ron Brew, a son of Mrs. J. Brew, of Orangeville. Ron, who has spent the last nine years in North Queensland, is a member of the Queensland contingent of the 2nd A.I.F. encamped at Rutherford, N.S.W., and was home on week-end leave. The committee, who had no provision made for this unexpected arrival, rose to the occasion and called on Mr. W. Angilley to make a cash presentation on behalf of the gathering. It was accompanied with the usual honours. Pte. Brew suitably responded, and dancing was resumed. Winners of the spot dance were Mrs. N. Mackie and Mr. J. Murdoch Snr., and the Monte Carlo went to Miss Shepard and Mr. Wal Dunbar. Master Jack Roberts entertained the gathering with a song, "Popeye the Sailor Man." Much thanks is due to Miss Cannan and Mr. Jim Kennedy who supplied the music (piano and violin) which helped to make the evening a success. The singing of the National Anthem terminated a very happy evening.[11]

Colin Tate
Flight Sergeant 428810

Enlisted:	Royal Australian Air Force, 10 Oct 1942, Sydney, NSW
Unit:	640 Squadron
Born:	21 February 1917, Randwick, NSW
Parents:	Cecil Tate & Theresa Little
Occupation:	Newsagent
Spouse:	Gwenneth Taplin; Married: 18 April 1942 St. John's C/E Camden
Next of Kin:	Gwennyth Tate
Died:	Killed in Action over Germany 30th January 1944
Buried:	Harrowgate (Stonefall) Cemetery, Yorkshire, U K
Roll of Honour:	Camden, NSW

Tate, Colin

Camden News Thursday 10 February 1944, page 1

Roll of Honour

The sympathy of the community was extended to Mrs. Colin Tate and Mrs. Tess Tate on Thursday evening last, when news was received that Flight Sgt. Colin Tate had been killed. The Minister for Air wired Mrs. Tate junr. that he regretted to inform her that her husband A428810 Flight Sergt. Colin Tate R.A.A.F. met his death during air operations. From facts known he was a member of a crew of Hallifax Bombers detailed to attack Berlin, Germany, on the 30th January. Owing to one engine cutting out the machine crashed at Cattfoss Lane, United Kingdom. The Minister for Air "joins with you in your time of bereavement and extends his sympathy."

Colin was a native of N.S.W., the only son of Mrs. T. Tate of Hill St., Camden, and the late Cecil Tate, and was 26 years of age. He was educated at Kings School Parramatta, and his early manhood days were spent in Camden where he was a familiar figure, popular among all. Shortly before enlisting he married Miss Gwen Taplin, only daughter of Mr. and Mrs. H. V. Taplin of Camden, to whom deep sympathy is extended. On enlisting Colin was a R.A.A.F. Reservist, and spent two months in the army before being called to the R.A.A.F. on the entry of Japan into the war. His training experience was gained at stations in N.S.W. and South Australia, from where he went to England through the United States and Canada. Records show that he had previous to his death, taken active part in raids over Germany [12].

Colin Tate

Leonard Suttor Wills

Warrant Officer Class 2 NX9229

Enlisted:	Australian Army, 20 December 1939 Paddington, NSW
Unit:	8 Motor Ambulance Convoy
Born:	13 February 1908 Gunnedah, NSW
Parents:	Percy Henry Wills & Clara Mona Suttor
Occupation:	Truck driver
Spouse:	– Clara Wills
	– 1952 Burwood, NSW Vera Alice Godfrey
Residence:	Rossmore, NSW
Next of Kin:	Clara Wills
Discharged:	14 September 1945
Died:	11 October 1961 Port Macquarie, NSW

Wills, Leonard Suttor

Camden News Thursday 29 February 1940, page 2

SOCIAL AT ROSSMORE

A large and representative gathering of residents of Bringelly and Rossmore was present at an evening on the 17th inst., given by the Wills family of Rossmore, in honour of the son, Leonard Suttor Wills, who was the first lad from the district to sail overseas, joining the 2/1 Field Ambulance. Owing to the short final leave that Leonard had before sailing it was impossible to have the evening before, so it was decided to hand the presentation to his mother to forward on. Mr. Young, of Rossmore, made the presentation, which took the form of a cheque.

The Wills family have been residents of Rossmore for many years and have always worked for the good of Australia. Len's grandmother was awarded one of King George V Jubilee Medals, his grandfather was "Father" of the famous Kangaroo's Rifle Club, and led them to many a stirring contest against the picked teams of the State, and his uncle and many of his relatives fought in the Great War, so we are sure that Len will carry on his family's good work and be "one grand soldier" for Australia.

During the evening Len's dog, which he had reared from a puppy, decided he would also like to be in the proceedings, so wandered into the hall and stayed for the rest of the evening.

Music for the dance was supplied by Grimson & Ollis' orchestra, and Mr. King, President of the Bringelly P. & C. Association, acted as M.C. Supper, which was enjoyed by all, was supplied by the ladies of Bringelly-Rossmore.[13]

War in the Mediterranean and the Middle East

Australian's units were active in North Africa, the Mediterranean area, and the Middle East between 1940 and 1942.

Royal Australian Navy ships saw action against the Italian navy from 1940 and supported Australian troops at Tobruk, often under heavy attack from the German Luftwaffe.

Australian troops were sent to the Middle East early in 1941. They took part in the ill-fated, politically motivated campaign to defend Greece and Crete and with many thousands captured by the Germans. They successfully defeated the Italian troops at Benghazi and Vichy French forces in Syria. With their allies they held off repeated and determined attacks on the port of Tobruk. They took the German insult of 'rats' in their holes and wore the title 'Rats of Tobruk' with pride. In 1942 Australians were prominent in the defeat of the Germans at the Battle of El Alamein.

In 1942 most troops were recalled to defend Australia against the Japanese. Units of the Navy and Air force remained in Europe until the end of the war. Many Australians served with the RAF and Royal Navy with several hundred fatalities.

Edward Allen Davis

Private NX7738

Enlisted:	Australian Army 7 November 1939 Paddington, NSW
Unit:	16th Garrison Battalion
Born:	22 September 1905 Sydney, NSW
Parents:	William Benjamin Davis & Sarah Annie Eggelton
Spouse:	Harriette Olive O'Berg; Married: 1956 Sydney, NSW
Residence:	Theresa Park, NSW
Next of Kin:	Frederick Davis
Discharged:	3 February 1945

Davis, Edward Allen

Camden News Thursday 21 January 1943, page 4

Mr. F. Sedgwick of Campbelltown, last week received a Christmas gift from Pte. Allen Davis of Theresa Park, which was posted at an advanced action station in the Tobruk area North Africa. Strange to say the parcel was wrapped up in two copies of The Camden News, the only paper he had available.[14]

William Allan Evans

Driver NX15070

Enlisted:	Australian Army 21 May 1940 Paddington, NSW
Unit:	2 Australian Artillery Training Regiment
Born:	24 January 1919 Stockton, NSW
Parents:	Christmas Evans & Mary Morgan
Spouse:	Elizabeth Ann Hird; Married: 1959 Chatswood, NSW
Residence:	Canterbury, NSW
Next of Kin:	Christmas Evans
Discharged:	11 September 1946
Died:	25 December 1988 Marrickville, NSW

Evans, William Allan

Camden News Thursday 8 Jan 1942, page 1

FROM THE FRONT

Mr. and Mrs. C. Evans, of Broughton Street, Camden, have received word from their son Sergt. Allan Evans, A.I.F. abroad. After months of silence he wrote saying he was sorry that he had not written before, but he had been away from his base for some time, and so had not received any mail nor had he written any. "Since I last wrote I have been to the following places: Tel Avin, Jerusalem, Naples, Nazareth, Cairo1, Alexandria, Haifer, Bezcouth and Asmara in Abyssinia, so you can see my duty has given me a fair run around.

"At present I am in hospital recovering from a fall I had the other day in Jerusalem.

"From the wing where I am, I can get three very fine views, one across the hills to the Dead Sea, another onto the mountains, where on a clear day eleven Arab villages can clearly be discerned. On the third side we have Jerusalem, this view leaves an impression that one will never forget. There is no real beauty, but the contrast of modern tall buildings on the skyline to the dull squat old fashioned buildings on the foreground is so sharp that the scene becomes unforgettable.

"Tel Avin is a modern town-full of refugees, just like King's Cross, but none the less interesting. There are two quarters, Jaffa the Arab quarters, and Tel Avin the Jewish. The place is very pretty, plenty of park space and trees; the streets are lined with modern shops and cafes whose owners charge exorbitant prices for all they sell. In these cafes one meets some very fine people mostly Czechs, Poles and other refugees whose lives have been wrecked by Hitler and his hordes. Quite a few of them are musicians and play in the cafes — they can play too, putting all their heart and soul into it. Money does not last long here, especially if one drinks. The chaps that I know don't drink thank goodness, so we do have a little money to spend on leave,

"The winter is in full swing now bringing with its cold weather and rain. It is quite the coldest climate I have ever experienced. It seems very strange to think that back home you are all enjoying the surfing season. I have met some very fine people here. An Australian doctor, who is a specialist, has been very kind to me and has taken me out a fair deal. I also have met the American Consul General to whose home I am going for Christmas.

"I am just about sick of doing nothing, at the front there are at least shells flying around, but back here war doesn't seem at all real. In fact I am beginning to think that this country is the safest of all."[15]

Ernest Henry McGrath

Private NX54836

Enlisted:	Australian Army, 15 July 1940, Paddington, NSW
Unit:	2/3 Army Field Workshops AAOC
Born:	18 June 1909 Orange, NSW
Parents:	Ernest Millington McGrath & Hannah Frances Barnes
Occupation:	Blacksmith
Spouse:	Heather Irene Maudsley; Married: 1940 Petersham, NSW
Residence:	Camden, NSW
Next of Kin:	Heather McGrath
Discharged:	26 May 1941
Died:	Died of injuries accident Sinai Desert 26th May 1941
Buried:	Gaza War Cemetery, Israel A.C.12
Memorial:	St. John's C/E Camden, NSW
Roll of Honour:	Camden, NSW

McGrath, Ernest Henry

Camden News Thursday 26 June 1941, page 1

THE LATE Pte. E. McGRATH
ACCIDENTALLY KILLED

Mrs. McGrath is in receipt of a letter written by Capt. F. E. Cowle, A.I.F. abroad, concerning the circumstances of the death of her husband, Pte. Ernie McGrath, who was killed on the 25th May. During the course of personal references, Capt. Crowle writes:

"It is the saddest task that has yet befallen me to write you and tell you the circumstances of Ernie's Home Call. There is nothing that I can say that would adequately express to you the sense of loss that we, Ernie's comrades, feel. He had no doubt told you of the work on which we were engaged, and how hard we all had to work and the circumstances under which we were operating. It is sufficient to say that we were given a task and we more than fulfilled the high hopes that were held of us. Ernie more than did his share, the hours he worked when occasion demanded, would cause a union leader to turn purple, but he was always cheerful and willing, and when receiving commendation would say that what he was doing was what he left Australia for — to do a job of work.

"We were moving in convoy on the 25th May, 1941, and were halted for a few minutes on the side of the road at about 6.30 p.m. and another convoy of vehicles passed us going in the same direction. Four of these passed us and the fifth was a fair distance back and Ernie tried to pass in front of the truck to get back to his vehicle when he was hit by the front guard and the wheels passed over his lower abdomen. Immediately he was given medical attention, but he only lived for an hour, remaining conscious the whole period; he was talking to us and about you, but had no knowledge that he was so seriously hurt. He asked for a cup of tea, and a cigarette and was quite cheerful, and even apologised to me for the delay he thought he was causing.

"It was a very sad cavalcade that brought him into camp. He said to me a few minutes before he passed on. "I think I'll go to sleep," which he did, and I am happy in the knowledge that he sleeps with Him, and I am sure that that will bring comfort to you. "He knows. He loves. He cares."

"Ernie was buried at Gaza War Memorial Cemetery, and when occasion offers we will send you a photo of his grave.

"Last Sunday, (1st June) we held a small, simple service for his unit mates, and I have been asked to send you the enclosed £15, Aust., not that we think you need the money but just that we would like to be associated with you in some small measure.

"I had to go through all Ernie's kit and I selected all that I anticipated would be of interest to you, and also enclosed is an Egyptian note and a canteen order which Ernie had in his belt, I thought you would be more interested in them as they are, than in their monetary value. Please convey to Ernie's people our profound sympathy in your, and their and our sad loss, and rest assured that you have been and will be remembered in our prayers."

Signed on behalf of the personnel of the Seventh Recovery Section

Frank E. Crowle, Capt.[16]

Camden News Thursday 9 October 1941, page 5

LATE PTE. E. H. McGRATH

Mrs. McGrath is in receipt of a letter from the Red Cross Bureau for Wounder, Missing and Prisoners of War. Under date of 29th May, the Commissioner in the Middle East, wrote as follows: –

Pte. McGrath, E. H. (Deceased)

"The above soldier who was a member of No. 7 Recovery Section, 2/3 A.F.T. died on May 26th, 1941, in a convoy. He was buried at 8.30 a.m. on the following day at Gaza War Cemetery (grave AC12). His relatives may like to know he rests in the shade of an Australian gum tree. The sun was shining as on an Australian summer morning when the cortege moved into the cemetery. There were 60 in the gathering of comrades and firing party. Padre A. T. Pitt-Owen, Depot Bn., officiated. Padre Pitt-Owen belongs to Arncliffe N.S.W. The firing party was commanded by Capt. A. G. Suthers of 2/12 Bn., now attached to 18 Inf. Sng. Bn.

"Mr. McLachlan went to the funeral and took some photographs which it is thought might be passed on to relatives. Details of these photographs are:

"On road from 1A.G.H. cortege passing through guard of honour; Padre Pitt-Owen and Capt. A. G. Suthers leading the cortege; nearing the site of the grave, firing party in rear; and passing Cenotaph in Gaza Cemetery.

"The photographs mentioned are enclosed. We know you will be glad to have them."[17]

Errol Wallis Stevenson Williams

Captain 4014

Enlisted:	New Zealand Army
Unit:	19th Infantry Battalion, New Zealand Forces
Born:	23 September 1915, Christchurch, New Zealand
Parents:	Rev Owen Wallis Stevenson & Elsie Clara May Stevenson
Occupation:	Professional Soldier
Spouse:	Suzanne Jean Crookston; Married: 18 December 1939 Christ's College Chapel, Christchurch, NZ
Residence:	Trentham, Wellington, NZ
Next of Kin:	Mrs S. J. Williams, C/o Dr Crookston, Camden, NSW
Died:	28 November 1941 Killed in action Western Desert, North Africa
Buried:	Knightsbridge War Cemetery, Acroma, Libya
Honours:	Mentioned in Dispatches

Williams, Errol Wallis Stevenson

Errol Williams was a New Zealander who had trained as a cadet at Duntroon. He became acquainted with Doctor Crookston and his family in Camden and spent many weekends in the area during training. Suzanne, the eldest daughter, gave him a white Bull Terrier as a mascot in 1937 and he was named Major. Williams later became engaged to Suzanne and married her in New Zealand in December 1939 with dog Major forming part of the wedding party. Major has his own place in New Zealand military history with a book *The Four-Legged Major* by Graham Spencer preserving the story of a military mascot from World War II.

Tragically their happy life together was to be short lived as Williams and his battalion departed for Egypt in mid-February 1940 together with Major. Errol was killed in action in Libya 28 November 1941. Parts of two letters written to the Crookston family prior to his departure for Egypt are as follows:

Christ College
Page 9

I can't say much about the war. I am going with a battalion of the finest young men New Zealand can muster, we will only be a drop in the ocean but perhaps we can help in some small way. Life is cruel when such men must suffer the fate of a much shortened life – but there it is. There is and will be great and lasting friendships made – the very best qualities will be brought out under the hard conditions.

Whilst I am away the N.Z. Govt. such as it, is will help to keep a soldier's wife and I shall arrange to have it sent to Camden.

Should I not come back, my heart sickens at the thought, then I can die knowing the one I care for more dearly and love more deeply than life itself is in the hand of those that love her with that same deep love. But I pray that God will be kind to us and give us a chance to make some sort of a little mark in this sad world of ours.

With all our love and happiness to you all,
Errol.

Capt Errol Williams 4014
19 Inf. Bn. NZEF
9th September 1941

... I spent a week on leave in Cairo. Ten or eleven months of continuous duty had rather taken the stuffing out of me – like the "Straw Man" in the "Wizard of Oz". 2/Lt. Major[i] is more than well he is getting fat – most unmilitary.

On Thursday we are holding Brigade Sports – my company has a good representation in the Battalion team and even I have to run in the Company Commanders race !!!!

How is the garden? Dry! You would love some of the beautiful colouring of the flowers over in Egypt. The heat seems to bring out brilliant colours but very little scent. But I long for the green bush and hills of N.Z. – the running, sparkling cold mountain streams – sunshine without this strong glare which make our eyes permanently on guard. Oh for peace and home!

I love and admire you all.
Your loving
Errol

18 Infantry Battalion

---

[i] See entry for Major Williams below

Major Williams

Major No 1 Dog

Unit:	19th Infantry Battalion, New Zealand Forces
Born:	abt 1937 Camden, NSW
Occupation:	Mascot
Died:	died of pneumonia 17 December 1944 Rimini, Italy
Buried:	with full Military Honours Rimini, Italy

Williams, Major

Major was a white Australian Bull Terrier which was given as a mascot to Captain Williams by Suzanne Crookston of Camden in 1937 whilst Captain William was a Cadet training at Duntroon, Canberra, ACT. When Captain Williams returned to New Zealand in 1938 Major joined him.

Captain Williams was appointed to the Special Force then being formed and was subsequently appointed Adjutant of the 19th Infantry Battalion. When Major joined his master he was registered as No. 1 New Zealand Dog. Major was an important member of the wedding party when Captain Williams married Suzanne Jean Crookston at Christ's College Chapel, Christchurch, NZ on 18 December 1939.

Major with Lieut. J.E. May

In 1940 Captain Williams and Major were appointed to the Middle East forces and Major paraded through Wellington with his Unit prior to their departure. They arrived in Maadi, Egypt in February 1940 to undertake training prior to being deployed to the western desert. The 19th Battalion took part in the digging of the Baggush Box, a field fortification near Maaten Baggush.

It was a tented camp, dug under sand dunes and said to be bomb-proof, as a temporary billet for troops taking part in operations against the Italian invasion of Egypt.

Major then returned to Cairo with Captain Williams at the Middle East Officer Cadet Training Unit (OCTU) until the end of June 1941. Major was promoted to 2nd Lieutenant as part of the West Coast Company of 19th Infantry Battalion, New Zealand Forces under the command of Captain Williams. In August 1941 he went with the Company to the Canal Zone and then joined the battalion in Libya in November 1939. He was behind the lines when his master was killed in action during the advance on Ed Duda on 28 November 1941.

Major fretted after the death of Captain Williams and was placed in the care of Captain Bill Aiken and returned to Maadi. He was promoted to Lieutenant and then Captain before leaving with his unit for 3 months in Syria. However when the Germans advanced into Egypt in June 1942 Major, together with his unit, was recalled and he entered the line at El Alamein and in July received shrapnel wounds to the thigh.

He received medical attention in the field, given a field medical card, and evacuated to an Advanced Dressing Station and then back to Maadi.

In the meantime his keeper, Captain Aiken, had been taken prisoner so when Major returned to his unit it was to the care of Major Tony Everist. He was promoted to Major in September 1942. In February 1943 while training with his unit they were inspected by Lieutenant-General Bernard Freyberg, commander of the New Zealand Division and Major as usual wore his special jacket with unit colours and emblem. *"The general took note of Major's attendance: 'Ah, the old dog. You've been on every parade yet'."*

At the end of 1943 the unit sailed for Italy accompanied by Major and his new handler Lieutenant Steve Whitton. He served until 17 December 1944 when he died of pneumonia at Rimini, Italy. Major was buried with full military honours, however unfortunately his grave marker is now missing.

The grave of Major

Frederick Charles Woollams

Sergeant NX13717

Enlisted:	Australian Army, 16 May 1940, Paddington, NSW
Unit:	2/3 Battalion
Born:	10 August 1909, Stuart Town, NSW
Parents:	Charles Woollams & Susan Margaret Elizabeth Jeffery
Occupation:	Dairy Farmer
Spouse:	Alice Elizabeth Walker; Married: 1927 Camden, NSW
Residence:	Rossmore, NSW
Next of Kin:	Alice Woollams
Discharged:	21 September 1945
Died:	27 March 1972 Camden, NSW
Buried:	Camden General - Anglican

Woollams, Frederick Charles

Camden News Thursday 6 March 1941, page 3

Letters From the Front

Pte. F. C. Woollams, A.I.F. Abroad, in a letter to Mrs. Parker, Hon. Secretary of the Bringelly -Rossmore Comforts Fund, writes: —

"This is my first opportunity of writing a short letter of thanks and appreciation for the parcels that your Comforts Fund have sent to me. As you no doubt already know, we have been getting on with our job in the last few weeks, and moving long distances through the desert, often a considerable distance in advance of the main body of our transport, we have had little opportunity of obtaining extra comfort in the way of enjoyable food or clean comfortable clothes, which makes these things, when they arrive, all the more acceptable.

You might be interested to know that I carried your cake through the battle of Tobruk in my haversack, you can imagine that it made a welcome addition to beef and biscuits when we were able to have a rest and a meal after 14 hours' fighting.

I also want to thank you on behalf of my brother, Leo, who was evacuated to hospital before the socks and scarf arrived, fortunately did not receive a serious injury. I am expecting to see him back with us again any day now.

I would like to express my belief that the British Empire has nothing to fear so long as the British race is what it is, whatever tales of daring heroism may be told of them, they would not be more than the truth. This does not apply to individuals, but to everyone who is taking part. You people at home who are providing little extra comforts for us are our chief mainstay."

F. C. WOOLLAMS, 29/1/41.[18]

War in the Pacific

The war in the Pacific began unexpectedly at 8.00 a.m. (Pearl Harbour time) Sunday, 7 December 1941, when Japan launched two carrier-based surprise air attacks on warships of the United States Pacific Fleet lying at anchor in Pearl Harbor in Hawaii. The two successive attacks were unexpected and had not been preceded by a declaration of war. They took place while Japanese diplomats were in Washington discussing American concerns about continuing Japanese military aggression in East Asia. The Japanese diplomats used these discussions to distract America while Japan secretly positioned a powerful aircraft carrier striking force off the Hawaiian Islands.

The unexpected attack against the United States fleet, causing a heavy loss of American lives, had resulted in a furious reaction in the US. It also concerned British Prime Minister Winston Churchill that the US would divert its resources to fight Japan rather than giving priority to the defeat of Nazi Germany.

"We knew that the outrage at Pearl Harbor had stirred the people of the United States to their depths. The official reports and the Press summaries we had received gave the impression that the whole fury of the nation would be turned upon Japan. We feared lest the true proportion of the war as a whole might not be understood. We were conscious of a serious danger that the United States might pursue the war against Japan in the Pacific and leave us to fight Germany and Italy in Europe, Africa, and in the Middle East."[19]

Likewise, in his determination to defeat Germany, Churchill was prepared to abandon Australia to Japan. All British Empire forces had withdrawn from the Malay Peninsula to Singapore by 31 January 1942, with the loss of at least 700 Australian lives since 14 January 1942. On 8 February 1942, Japanese forces landed on the Island, and within 5 days, Singapore had fallen. More than 100,000 British Empire Troops (including an entire Australian division) became prisoners of war, and hundreds of European citizens were interred.

On 19 February 1942, Japanese fighters and bombers attacked the port and shipping in Darwin harbour twice the same day, resulting in the deaths of 252 Allied service personnel and civilians. Britain had been happy to accept all the soldiers, sailors and airmen that Australia was prepared to place at their disposal for the defence of Britain, but Churchill angrily castigated Australian Prime Minister John Curtin (who became Australia's 14th Prime Minister on 7 October 1941) when he withdrew Australian forces from the Mediterranean following the fall of Singapore.

Despite Churchill's objection, Curtin immediately withdrew all Royal Australian Navy ships from the Mediterranean theatre of war together with the 6th and 7th Divisions of the Australian Infantry Force. Whilst Curtin's priority was the defence of Australia, Churchill wanted the Australian troops to defend Burma and India against the advancing Japanese. However, on 9 March 1942, the Dutch surrendered the capital of the Dutch East Indies to Japan, effectively leaving Australia as the last bastion against Japan in the South-West Pacific. The capture of British Malaya, the British colonies in northern Borneo, and the Dutch East Indies had provided Japan with vast resources of oil, rubber, minerals and food.

Curtin appealed to the United States on 14 March 1942 for assistance in defending Australia.

"Australia is the last bastion between the west coast of America and the Japanese. If Australia goes, the Americas are wide open."

War in the Pacific

When General Douglas Macarthur arrived in Australia later the same month, Curtin learnt that Churchill had been lying to him when he had promised British support to oppose a Japanese invasion of Australia.

Australia declares war on Japan. The Governor General (Lord Gowrie) reading the proclamation announcing that Australia is at war with Japan. From left: The Secretary, Prime Minister's Department (Mr. F. Strahan) the Minister for the Army (Mr. Forde), the Prime Minister (Mr. Curtin) and Lord Gowrie

Edward James Booth

Private NX54448

Enlisted:	Australian Army, 25 June 1940, Paddington, NSW
Unit:	2/33 Australian Infantry Battalion
Born:	11 June 1910 Bexley, NSW
Parents:	Henry Robert Booth & Henrietta Matilda Penfold
Next of Kin:	Harry Booth
Died:	1 November 1943 of illness New Guinea
Buried:	Port Moresby Bomana War Cemetery Papua New Guinea
Roll of Honour:	Camden, NSW

Booth, Edward James

Camden News Thursday 20 January 1944, page 1

THE LATE TED BOOTH.

Mrs. J. Bond[i] of Camden, is in receipt of two letters from the war front having reference to the death of her brother, Pte. Ted Booth.

Capt. K. Power[ii] O/C A Coy. in expressing sympathy to Mrs. Bond in the loss of her brother, who died in New Guinea on 31st October last. "We were out on patrol," he writes, "and I noticed that Ted was not looking the best. I sent him back to Headquarters in charge of a Jap prisoner. He arrived back and reported to the medical officer after delivery of the Jap. The M.O. sent him to hospital. The next thing we heard was that Ted had passed away, not of malaria as we thought, but typhus. It came as a shock to me as I had already lost one of my old school mates in Percy Gander.[iii] Ted had been in my company for years and was known and liked by everyone in addition I used to live practically next door to him at Brownlow Hill."

Edward James Booth

Pte. Don Atfield[iv] of Camden, wrote saying: "Just a few lines to you regarding the death of your brother Ted, and my mate. It is with a heavy heart that I write, it was a terrible shock to me, so I can readily believe how you feel about Ted's death. He died with typhus on the 31st October, in the H.G.H. at Moresby. I met him in a medical dressing station while I was receiving treatment for fever, and Ted was here for a couple, of days. I had quite a good yarn to him, he seemed very well then, but took a relapse, and then we were informed of his passing. Ted was one of the finest men one could meet, and a great mate."[20]

---

[i] Charlotte Elizabeth Bond nee Booth wife of James Adam Bond a carrier. Her husband was honoured with a Chinese ceremony at his gravesite in Camden when he died 2 May 1944.
[ii] POWER, Captain Kevin 28087 (VX12699
[iii] GANDER, Horace Arthur (known as Percy) NX 50592
[iv] ATFIELD, Donald Albert, Private NX33635

Camden News Thursday 10 February 1944, page 1

PTE. EDWARD (TED) BOOTH

Pte. Edward (Ted) Booth died on the 31st October, 1943, whilst on Active Service in New Guinea. He was there stricken with typhus which proved fatal. He was 33 years of age, enlisting early in the war and participated with the AIF in the Middle East prior to their return in April 1942, to take place in the New Guinea campaign. He was a brother of Mrs. J. Bond of Camden, Alfred[i] of Bobs Range, Harold of Arncliffe, Mrs. E. Small of The Oaks, and Miss Hilda Booth of Sydney.[21]

---

[i] Alfred Joseph Lashma Booth

Francis Carling
Private NX24954

Enlisted:	Australian Army, 30 May 1941 Paddington, NSW
Unit:	2/1 Infantry Battalion
Born:	23 December 1915 Moss Vale, NSW
Parents:	John Stanislaus Carling & Margaret Henrietta Jones
Occupation:	Barman
Residence:	Camden, NSW
Next of Kin:	John Carling
Died:	5 December 1942 of wounds, New Guinea
Buried:	Port Moresby Bomana War Cemetery, Papua, New Guinea.
Roll of Honour:	Camden, NSW

Carling, Francis

Camden News Thursday 10 December 1942, page 1

DIED OF WOUNDS
FRANCIS CARLING

Mr. and Mrs. J. S. Carling of Elderslie, have received word from the Minister for the Army, that their son, Private Francis Carling, previously reported wounded in action, is now reported died of wounds on Saturday last, 5th December.

Pte. Carling was 27 years of age and enlisted in the A.I.F early in the war, seeing active service in the Middle East, participating in the September 1941 offensive. About four months ago he returned from North Africa, and for the past three months was with the Australian troops in New Guinea where he received his fatal wounds. "Frankie" was a keen member of the Elderslie Cricket Club.

Deep sympathy is expressed with his family.[22]

Francis Carling

Camden News Thursday 17 December 1942, page 4

Roll of Honour

Pte. Francis Carling died of wounds on Saturday, 5th December. Frank, who was 27 years of age, was a son of Mr. and Mrs. J. S. Carding of Elderslie. He enlisted in the A.I.F. early in the war, and saw service in the Middle East, participating in the September, 1941 offensive. About four months ago he returned from North Africa, and since then was with the Australian troops in New Guinea, where he received his fatal wounds.[23]

Harold Charles Chesham

Private NX121202 (N375219)

Enlisted:	Australian Army 27 August 1942 Michaels Camp, NSW
Unit:	2/2 Guard Battalion
Born:	20 June 1904 Camden, NSW
Parents:	John Chesham & Sarah Elizabeth Hoffmann
Residence:	Camden, NSW
Next of Kin:	John Chesham
Discharged:	26 February 1946
Died:	1966 Picton, NSW

Chesham, Harold Charles

NX121202
Private Chesham H
2/1 Guard Regiment

Dear Elsie,
Just a few lines wishing you a merry Christmas and a Happy New Year.
Dick[i]

---

[i] Editor: This note was included by Janice, but we do not understand the connection with Charles Chesham.

Jacqueline Crookston

Private NFX152931 (N392150) (NX152931)

Enlisted:	Australian Army, 22 March 1943, Charters Towers, QLD
Unit:	Australian Army Medical Womens Services
Born:	19 March 1919, Camden, NSW
Residence:	Camden, NSW
Next of Kin:	R. Crookston
Discharged:	21 June 1946
Note:	Her WWII service medals are in the Camden Museum collection.

Crookston, Jacqueline

During World War Two, Jacqueline joined the Voluntary Aid Detachment (VAD) in Camden and then enlisted in the Australian Army Medical Women's Service from 1942 to 1945 and saw service in New Guinea and the South-West Pacific. Her World War Two service medals are in the Camden Museum collection.

Camden News Thursday 29 April 1943

> Sad news has been received by Dr. and Mrs. Crookston of the death of Flying Officer Anthony Stewart, R.A.A.F., on service overseas. Flying Officer Stewart - was the fiance of Miss Jacqueline Crookston, who is away on service as a member of the A.A.M.W.S.[24]

New Guinea. At an Australian Field Hospital in New Guinea two members of the Australian Army Medical Women's Service (AAMWS) are on service. Lance Corporal J. Crookston of NSW, and Major Christie, adjust a tent flap while Corporal E. Maskell of Melbourne. Vic, and Private M. McVeigh of Young, NSW, look on.

Horace Arthur Gander

Private NX 50592

Enlisted:	Australian Army, 24 June 1940 Paddington, NSW
Unit:	2/33 Australian Infantry Battalion
Born:	01 July 1908 Perthville, NSW
Parents:	Albert John Gander & Lucia (Lucy) Anne Daley Cole
Residence:	Camden, NSW
Next of Kin:	Lucia Gander
Died:	11 October 1943 Lae, New Guinea
Buried:	Lae War Cemetery, Papua New Guinea
Roll of Honour:	Camden, NSW

Gander, Horace Arthur

Camden News Thursday 10 February 1944, page 1

PTE. HORACE GANDER

News was received in Camden on 1st November, 1943, that NX50592 Pte. Horace Gander had been killed in action in New Guinea on the 11th October. Percy, as he was so well known locally, was 35 years of age, and was born in Camden. He was the second son of Mr. and Mrs. Albert Gander, of 40 Cowper Street, Randwick, and formerly well-known residents of Camden. Horace enlisted locally early in 1940, and left some few months later with the 7th Division A.I.F., and was on Active Service in the Middle East and the Syrian Campaign prior to returning to Australia in April 1942. Since then he had been on Active Service in New Guinea.[25]

Horace Gander

Harold William Smart

Sapper N375466

Enlisted:	Australian Army, 22 January 1942, Camden, NSW
Unit:	7 Field Company
Born:	20 July 1913 Camden, NSW
Parents:	Charles Thomas Smart & Ada Adelaide Munday
Occupation:	Shop assistant
Spouse:	– Leta Margaret Jane McLung
	– Lillian Pearl Smart
Residence:	Camden, NSW
Next of Kin:	Leta Smart
Discharged:	24 July 1946
Died:	21 February 1991 Camden, NSW
Buried:	Cawdor Uniting
Note:	On 2 November 1945 sustained a traumatic amputation of the right hand. Caused by a premature explosion of one stick of gelignite and 6 inches of safety fuse

Smart, Harold William

Camden News Thursday 1 November 1945, page 4

A report has been received from Bougainville Is. that Spr. Harold Smart, A.I.F., son of Mr. and Mrs. C. T. Smart, Park Street, Camden, met with a serious accident to his hand while using explosives.[26]

On the Home Front

Following Pearl Harbour, the Australian Government recognised that Darwin was vulnerable to attack. On 16th December 1941, an official order was issued by the Administrator to evacuate women and children from the city. The civilian population were given less than 24 hours' notice and were allowed only minimal luggage. The majority of the 1,066 women and 900 children went by sea, with the first group leaving Darwin on the *Koolinda* on 19th December. The troop carriers *Zealandia*, *USS President Grant*, *Montoro*, and *Koolama* also evacuated civilians with the last ship sailing on 15th February just before the bombing of Darwin. Others left by plane, road and train.

The Australian Government developed Darwin's military ports and airfields, built coastal batteries and anti-aircraft guns and steadily enlarged its garrison of troops. The preparations were essential. Japan recognised that Darwin was a key port for the Allied ships, planes and forces defending the Dutch East Indies (now Indonesia and East Timor).

War came to Australia's shore on 19th February 1942 when 188 Japanese planes attacked Darwin, whose harbour was packed with 46 allied ships. The Japanese had conducted a reconnaissance flight on 10th February when there were 27 ships in the harbour and 30 aircraft on the civilian and military airfields. The attack on 19th February was the largest attack since Pearl Harbour.

On 3rd March 1942, the Western Australian town of Broome came under attack; Australia's second-worst air raid.

The Japanese continued to target Darwin, Western Australia and Queensland over the next 20 months, including the raid on Townsville, Katherine, Wyndham, Derby and Port Hedland. In late 1942, three raids were made against Townsville (Queensland) as well as Millingimbi (Northern Territory) and four raids on the Exmouth Gulf.

Following attacks on Pearl Harbour, concerns were raised about possible attacks on Sydney. In December 1941, the following message was relayed:-

"In view of the possibility of an attempt by submarines to enter the Harbour duty vessels and patrols have been arranged as follows daily between 1900K and 0900K.

Duty A/S vessel on A/S stationary patrol in the loop area. Duty M/S vessel at immediate notice in Watsons Bay. One coastal patrol boat and four Naval Auxiliary Patrol Boats patrolling between LADY BAY and CANNAE POINT. K.D.C. is to immediately inform all duty vessels of any unidentified signature on the loops. Duty M/S vessel is then to proceed to the West Channel and attempt to intercept the submarine. Depth Charges in S.P. Bos and Duty M/S vessels are to be set to 100 feet."

These preparations were to prove essential as Sydney came under attack from Japanese submarines in May 1942. Five large Japanese submarines positioned themselves 52 kilometres north-east of Sydney Heads on the night of 29th May and the following day launched a reconnaissance aircraft that circled Sydney Harbour. The pilot reported the presence of battleships and cruisers moored in the harbour. The next night three mini-submarines were launched to penetrate the harbour defences and sink the ships at anchor.

The presence of the submarines, the first entered the harbour at 8:00 p.m., went undetected until one of them became entangled in the anti-submarine nets suspended between George's Head and Green Point. Once the alarm was raised, *HMAS Yarroma* opened fire, damaging the first submarine; the Japanese crew then activated demolition charges which destroyed the submarine and killed them.

At about 9:45 p.m., a second submarine entered the harbour and headed west towards the Harbour Bridge. The submarine was approximately 200 metres from Garden Island when it was fired on by the USS *Chicago*, which missed its target. The submarine fired two torpedoes at the USS *Chicago* but missed its target, with one torpedo running ashore on Garden Island and failing to explode. The second torpedo passed under the Dutch submarine *K9* striking the harbour bed beneath *HMAS Kuttabul*, where it exploded, killing 21 sailors. This Japanese submarine then slipped out of the harbour.

HMAS Yandra sighted the third submarine at the entrance to the harbour, and it was depth-charged but not sunk as some four hours later it entered the harbour. It was subsequently detected by Royal Australian Navy vessels, depth charges and sunk in Taylor Bay. The Japanese crew committed suicide.

The five mother submarines embarked on a campaign to disrupt merchant shipping in eastern Australian waters. Over the next month, the submarines attacked at least seven merchant vessels, sinking three ships and killing 50 sailors. During this period, the submarines bombarded the ports of Sydney and Newcastle.

On the morning of 8th June 1942, two of the submarines bombarded Sydney and Newcastle. The submarine's commander ordered the gun crew to target the Sydney Harbour Bridge with ten shells fired over a four-minute period. Nine of the shells landed in the Eastern Suburbs, and one landed in the water. The submarine then crash-dived to prevent successful retaliation by coastal artillery batteries. Only one shell detonated, and the only injuries inflicted were cuts and fractures from falling bricks or broken glass when the unexploded shells hit buildings.

The second submarine shelled Newcastle from 9 km north-east of Stockton Beach. The submarine fired 34 shells over 16 minutes, including eight star shells with the target being the BHP steelworks. However, the shells landed over a large area, causing minimal damage and no fatalities: the only shell to detonate damaged a house on Parnell Place, while an unexploded shell hit a tram terminus. Fort Scratchley returned fire, the only time an Australian land fortification has fired on an enemy warship during wartime, but the submarine escaped unscathed.

Italian youths gaoled

Camden News Thursday 7 May 1942, page 3

Damage at Liverpool Mill
ITALIAN YOUTHS GAOLED

At Liverpool Police Court on Monday of last week, Vinvenco Viglione, 18, and Camelo Anastasio, 17, both Italians, described as enemy aliens, pleaded guilty to a charge of impeding production by deliberately rolling a gear wheel into the power switchboard at the Manchester Weaving Mills, Liverpool, on January 16.

Mr. Collins, S.M., sentenced each to imprisonment for three months and said he would recommend that when their sentences expired they be interned for the duration of the war.

Const. Noble said, in evidence, that in a statement made to the police, Viglione had said that Anastasio told him how to put the switchboard out of order by rolling a steel gear wheel along a concrete platform until it struck the board. Viglione said that they had conceived the idea of damaging the switchboard in order to procure a spell for about half an hour until repairs were made.

As a result of the dislocation of the switch gear, 20 other employees and eight machines were stopped, and about two hours' production was lost. — "Liverpool News."[27]

Baron Frederick Elliott von Frankenberg

Camden News Thursday 6 April 1950, page 1

BARON F. E. von FRANKENBERG

Frederick Elliott von Frankenberg und Ludwigsdorf, residing at Spring Hills, Glenmore, passed away on Thursday, March 30. He had been in the Camden district since 1928 after he bought his property from Mr. A. L. Bennett. He was born on 2nd January, 1889 at St. Paul, Minnesota, U.S.A., his father having migrated to America as early as 1866 with his parents. His mother was Jessie Elliott, daughter of Fred Elliott, one of the founders of Elliott Bros, now incorporated in Drug Houses of Australia. His parents decided to give their only son a German education, for which reason they migrated back to Germany in 1897. Owing to this, Mr. von Frankenberg joined the German Army previous to any idea of the first world war and became an officer. This move got him into the first world war against the Allies, but realising his international relationship, and having always the best intentions, he managed to get discharged from the Army in the beginning of 1915, and subsequently went to Switzerland where he became a Swiss-national. In 1927 he travelled to Australia where he met his present wife, Olive Ward Taylor, the daughter of Mr. John Taylor, a city alderman. Five years after his arrival in Australia he became a naturalized British subject.

Baron F. E. von Frankenberg

On the death of his mother in 1927 the Baron and Baroness von Frankenberg travelled via Java to Switzerland to arrange the inheritance on that side. On his return he took up the title of Baron, which is of ancient Austrian origin, the family having originated in Silesia, then an Austrian province. His direct ancestor was Abraham von Frankenberg und Ludwigsdorf, the mystic biographer of Jacob Boehme in the then Duchy of Oels, who was renowned for his remark to the question put by his Duke Henry, "Frankenberg what religion are you?" "Ego sum cor omnium religeonum" meaning "I am the heart of all religions." Baron von Frankenberg followed this epithet in his own life, as he was christened in the Church of England, confirmed in the Lutheran Church, married in the Presbyterian, and attended the Methodist Church locally, and also that he as early at 1925 joined the Sufi Order of Inayat Khan, which holds to the essential unity of truth in all religions. He has since represented this teaching in Australia, and this in fact is what constituted his life's work.

Apart from the Sufi Order, the Baron became interested in Free Masonry and ultimately became First Principal of the Royal Arch Chapter Campbelltown, No. 528 S.C. in October, 1949, which rank he held at his death. Other orders of Freemasonry of which he was an active member were: the Order of the Temple, The Knights of Malta, Royal Ark Mariners and Knights of the Babylonish Pass, as well as the Cryptic Council Degree Orders.[28]

Andrew William Macarthur-Onslow

Flight Lieutenant 261535

Enlisted:	Royal Australian Air Force
Unit:	7 Service Flying Training School Deniliquin
Born:	28 December 1917 Sydney, NSW
Parents:	Francis Arthur Macarthur-Onslow & Sylvia Seton Chisholm
Next of Kin:	Sylvia Macarthur-Onslow
Died:	18 January 1943 aircraft crash, Curraburula, NSW
Buried:	Tamworth War Cemetery. Row A. Grave 6
Roll of Honour:	Camden, NSW
Notes:	Sergeant Dawson 405724 and Flight Lieutenant MacArthur-Onslow 261535 (former s/no 1535) were killed in the loss of Wirraway A20-45 near Curralubula, NSW

Macarthur-Onslow, Andrew William

Camden News Thursday 21 January 1943, page 4

Sad news was received on Monday of the death of Flight Lieutenant Andrew Macarthur Onslow, R.A.A.F. killed in an operational flight that day near Tamworth. Sergeant Thomas Myles Dawson, of Mareeba, North Queensland, who accompanied Pilot Officer Macarthur-Onslow, was also killed. Andrew, the youngest son of Mrs. Sylvia Onslow, of "Mount Gilead," was 25 years of age, and had for some time been on service with the R.A.A.F. His sister, Mrs. Michael King, Ingleburn, and Miss Macarthur Onslow, Gilbulla, Menangle, with others representing the family attended the funeral on Tuesday.[29]

Andrew Macarthur-Onslow

Camden News Thursday 11 February 1943, page 1

Flight Lieutenant Andrew Macarthur Onslow

As previously reported Flight Lieut. Andrew Macarthur Onslow was killed in an aircraft accident at Tamworth on 18th January, 1943. He was the youngest son of the late Mr. F. A. Macarthur Onslow and Mrs. Onslow, and was born at Camden in 1917. He was educated at Tudor House and Cranbrook.

On leaving school he completed a wool classing course at the Sydney Technical College, and with the Commonwealth Wool and Produce Company, Sydney.

F/Lieut. Andrew Macarthur Onslow was interested in light car racing and competed in the Monte Carlo Rally and other road events in England. He learned to fly with the Royal Aero Club, Sydney, and completed his training as a commercial pilot and instructor with his service training in England. In 1938 he flew his own survey plane from England to Australia, where he formed a company called Air Travel and Survey, carrying out Government survey contracts throughout the Commonwealth.

On the Home Front

In 1935 he joined the Royal New South Wales Lancers gaining his commission in 1937. At the outbreak of war he transferred to the Royal Australian Air Force, where he has since served as an instructor.[30]

Doreen Grace Wilkinson, nee Malcolm

Lance Corporal NF453186

Enlisted:	Australian Army, 9 March 1943, Paddington, NSW
Unit:	Australian Womens Army Service
Born:	3 February 1925, Camden, NSW
Residence:	Cobbitty, NSW
Next of Kin:	Elsie Malcolm
Discharged:	24 December 1945
Died:	9 February 2019
Buried:	St Paul's Anglican Church, Cobbitty NSW
Note:	OAM awarded in 2004 for community service. 'For service to the community, particularly through the Camden Show Society'.; The Camden Museum holds her two-piece army uniform and the miniatures of her medals, for her AWAS service in World War II and the miniature for her OAM

Wilkinson nee Malcolm, Doreen Grace

Camden News Sunday 14 November 1937, page 6

There were two candidates of the Cobbitty Public School sitting for the Primary Final Examination, and both had successful passes. They were Doreen Malcolm and Percy J. Hore.[31]

Camden Historical Society Newsletter Winter 2010, page 3

Cobbitty's Finest Hour

On Friday 4 June 2010 at 6 p.m. the book '*Cobbitty's Finest Hour*' written by Donald Howard will be launched at the Camden Museum, 40 John Street, Camden. The book is Donald's reminiscences of his boyhood in the quiet village of Cobbitty during the Second World War, including some humorous memories of the 'Battle for Cobbitty'. The book will be launched by Mrs Doreen Wilkinson OAM who grew up with Donald, and when she was a girl rode her bike from Cobbitty to Camden during the same years as Donald.

Doreen Wilkinson nee Malcolm

Marie Celeste Sidman

Aircraftwoman 106458

Enlisted:	Royal Australian Air Force 28 September 1942 Sydney, NSW
Unit:	Garbutt
Born:	2 September 1924 Burwood, NSW
Parents:	Robert Alfred Sidman & Jean Elizabeth Tyson nee MacIntosh
Occupation:	Shop assistant
Residence:	Campbelltown, NSW
Next of Kin:	Robert Sidman
Discharged:	6 March 1946

Sidman, Marie Celeste

Camden News Thursday 27 September 1945, page 5

J-V DAY
VICTORY CELEBRATIONS FROM A NEW ANGLE

Well, it's all over now!

It's so marvellous that I still can't believe that the war has finally come to an end.

I'm sure you all had a marvellous time down there.... still I couldn't have asked for much more up here. (I am at Garbutt on weather signals at the aerodrome, 5 miles from Townsville, and we certainly had a "wow" of a time; as a. matter of fact I am still getting over it.

I was working at the actual time when word came through, but luckily at 8.45 a.m. on the 15th August, I had a few minutes' break, so changed frequency on my Set to listen to a bit of music. Just as I changed over, it was announced that Mr. Attlee, England's P.M. was going to make a statement, so I called all in, to listen in to it. Of course, after the first sentence was spoken, everyone shouted with joy, but soon settled down to hear the rest of the speech. By that, time the room was practically full (Officers included) and at the end of the speech was played the National Anthem, and everyone in the room stood to attention. A couple of them had hats on, and of course saluted. Everyone was so still and silent, it was hard to realise that only a few minutes previously everyone had been so excited. Never before has our National Anthem meant so much to me, and never before have I ever felt so proud that I am an Australian doing my bit in such a big job. I'm afraid I was a bit silly, because instead of rejoicing with the rest after the playing of the National Anthem, I went outside and had quite a good cry. I just couldn't help thinking of all those thousands of prisoners who have suffered so much for so long. Still I came back to earth after a while, and went mad with the rest of the crowd. Of course bottles came from nowhere at all, so very soon everyone was drinking, singing and dancing.

During the afternoon I was able to manage a 2-hour break on my watch and went into town (Townsville) to join in the fun. The streets were covered with everything from coloured streamers to toilet paper (mostly the latter), and there were thousands of people doing the craziest of things. Somehow I found myself in a Jeep with another lass, going up and down the main street screaming wildly and waving to everyone.

On the night of the 15th August, there was a great procession through the city, and a few other girls and myself marched with the A.I.F. We were singing all the way, and believe me "Pack Up Your Troubles" got a heck of a bashing. There were several bands including a Pipe band, and also a Chinese band. The floats were beautiful, and very original. There was one built into the shape of a small ship with all the details, it even had Signal Flags spelling the word "Victory." It was estimated by the police that there were approximately 36,000 people lining the streets, and about 1,000 taking part in the procession. Every light in the City was on, and all the Neon lights were blazing. Coloured rockets shot through the air all night, and along the water front in every tree were beautiful fairy lights.

106458, W.A.A.A.F.[32]

Jean Weir

Sergeant NF446183

Enlisted:	Australian Army, 29 December 1942, Paddington, NSW
Unit:	Australian Womens Army Service
Born:	2 February 1922 Bankstown, NSW
Parents:	David Weir & Ethel Readford
Spouse:	Donald Evans Sherlock; Married: 1952 Methodist Camden, NSW
Residence:	Camden, NSW
Next of Kin:	David Weir
Discharged:	31 January 1946

Weir, Jean

The Daily Telegraph Thursday 20 October 1949, page 16

Girl Art Students In Hyde Park Exhibition

Six girls and 60 ex-servicemen will exhibit paintings today in the first big Australian open-air art show to take place in Hyde Park, Sydney.

With the ex-servicemen students the girls are studying art under the Commonwealth Reconstruction Training Scheme at the Technical College.

Known as the Strath Art Group, the men and women students formerly studied at a branch of the Technical College in Strathfield.

The girls are ex-W.A.A.A.F.S. Rene Beckley and Cynthia Muller, ex-A.W.A.S., Jean Weir, June Felthan, and Betty Drew, and ex-W.R.A.N. Vi Hainsworth.

Some of the girls hope to go abroad at the end of this year, when they will have completed three years' training under the C.R.T.S.

Others will take the extra two years' course at the College to graduate.

Rene Beckley, who before the war was a member of the art staff of her father's stained-glass factory, said that she would eventually go abroad.

"I want to finish the five years' course and then teach to earn enough for a trip overseas," Rene said.

Miss Beckley was a teleprinter operator in the W.A.A.A.F

Cynthia Muller, of Western Australia, plans to marry Bill Sweeney, a former C.R.T.S. student in illustration at the Tech.

They will leave for Europe next year on a "working" holiday.

Miss Muller said that she hoped to visit relatives in Norway.

One of the most versatile of the group, she worked as a commercial artist before the war, and was an electrician in the W.A.A.A.F. She also in structed in the service in English and mathematics.

Jean Weir will leave for Scotland next year to stay with relatives. She plans to study art in Italy and France.

Rene Beckley 's varied exhibits in today's show include an etching of the front entrance to the London Arcade, Perth, an oil painting of a King's Cross, scene, a painting with design based on aborigine motifs, and the interior of a room in her own flat.

"The aim of the Strath Group is to hold an exhibition in Hyde Park, Sydney, once a year," Miss Beckley said.

"Any members abroad could send exhibits back to Australia," she added.

Mr. Charles Lloyd Jones will open today's exhibition at 2.15 p.m.

The past six months have meant constant preparation for the students, who have completed their exhibits between classes at the College.

The selection, committee included artists William Dobell, Hal Missingham, Douglas Dundas, and Wallace Thornton.

The students spent hours yesterday preparing the park site for the exhibition opposite David Jones', Elizabeth Street.

Today. they will arrange 136 exhibits and will later work in rosters to show visitors around the exhibition.[33]

GIRL ARTISTS who will exhibit in the Strath Art Group's open-air show in Hyde Park today (from left) June Feltham, Jean Weir, Rene Beckley, Cynthia Muller, and Vi Hainsworth. They are C.R.T.S students at the Technical College, Darlinghurst.

Prisoners of War

Camden News Thursday 19 June 1941, page 2

DIGEST OF WAR NEWS
Air Mail Letter Cards

Members of the A.I.F. in the Middle East will shortly be able to communicate with home by air mail at a cost of threepence. In announcing this, the Army Minister (Mr. P. Spender) said that the Post Office had agreed to proposals put forward by the A.I.F. under which special air mail letter cards could be forwarded from the troops in the Middle East to Australia by air mail at a cost of three pence each The letter cards will be made available to the troops without charge.[34]

Camden News Thursday 30 July 1942, page 4

REPORTED MISSING

Official notification by the Defence Department has been issued of certain members of the A.I.F. as reported missing. Among the lists were the following local soldiers: —

W. Chapman, of Narellan, later residing at Leichhardt ;

Colin Chapman, of The Oaks ;

Orchard Gunn, of Camden Park ;

A.J. Carvith, of Narellan, where his wife and two children are now in residence;

Eric G. Kelloway, son of the Mayor and Mayoress of Camden Ald. H. S. and Mrs. Kelloway ;

Colin Dengate, of Cawdor, grandson of Mr. and Mrs. E. J. Dengate ;

Leo Clark, Bimlow, grandson of Mr. and Mrs. M. P. Maxwell.[35]

Camden News Thursday 20 August 1942, page 3

WHEN WRITING TO PRISONERS OF WAR

Owing to the work entailed by attending to prisoners of war mail service for our prisoners in Japanese hands next of kin are asked to take particular care in addressing their letters. They are advised as follows: —

Do be careful to write the sender's name and address on the back of the envelope.

Do write clearly.

Do use Red Cross message service for non-interned civilians.

Do include for civilian internees the last known address.

Don't enclose another letter with a prisoner's letter.

Don't send more than one sheet of paper. Writing may be on both sides.

Don't enclose any stamps for letters to prisoners of war in Japanese hands.

Don't write more than once a month for the present. There is no air mail to the Far East Airmail service (1/- for letters and 6d for postcards) is only available for prisoners of war in Europe.

Attention to these details may make all the difference between the prisoner of war receiving his letters from home, and the keen disappointment of mail having gone astray through incorrect addressing, or other reasons.[36]

David Rose Payten

Gunner NX3292

Enlisted:	Australian Army, 25 October 1939 Paddington, NSW
Unit:	2/3 Field Regiment
Born:	12 September 1918 Campbelltown, NSW
Parents:	Arthur Granville Payten & Jessie Muriel Horniman
Residence:	Campbelltown, NSW
Next of Kin:	Arthur Payten
POW:	Prisoner of Germany
Died:	28 September 1941 Illness Stalag, Germany
Buried:	Durnbach War Cemetery Germany

Payten, David Rose

Camden News Thursday 18 September 1941, page 4

Mr. and Mrs. A. G. Payten, of Sydney Road, Campbelltown, have at last received official news from their son, Gunner David Payten, to the effect that he is now a prisoner of war somewhere in Germany. Gunner Payten was one of the many who was unable to be evacuated from Crete.[37]

Camden News Thursday 27 November 1941, page 4

Gunner David Rose Payten, eldest son of Mr. and Mrs. A. G. Payten, of Campbelltown, who was recently reported to be a prisoner of war in Germany, died on the 26th September from illness in a German prison camp. The shock of his death came as a stunning blow to his parents and the whole populace of Campbelltown where he was born. Mr. and Mrs. Payten's second son is also abroad on active service. We join our numerous readers in expressing sincerest of sympathy to the bereaved family.[38]

Max Ian Wheatley
Major NX12343 (N60116)

Enlisted:	Australian Army, 8 May 1940, Paddington, NSW
Unit:	2/2 Machine Gun Battalion
Born:	7 April 1915, Goulburn, NSW
Parents:	Willie Roy Wheatley & Myra May Levy
Occupation:	Professional Soldier
Residence:	"Bellevue" Rossmore, NSW
Next of Kin:	Roy Wheatley
Discharged:	13 October 1945
POW:	Prisoner of Italy
Died:	28 April 1993
Honours:	Mentioned in Dispatches

Wheatley, Max Ian

Camden News Thursday 17 September 1942, page 4

Major Max Wheatley of Rossmore. and Capt. W. M. Stephens, formerly of Appin, previously reported missing, are now known to be prisoners of war in Italy. Their names appear in a list submitted by the Vatican.[39]

Camden News Thursday 10 February 1944, page 1

MAJOR MAX WHEATLEY
PRISONER OF WAR RETURNS

It is pleasing to know that Major Max Wheatley, son of Mr. and Mrs. Roy Wheatley of Rossmore, has returned home after a trying experience as a prisoner of war in Italy for over twelve months.

Soon after the Australian Ninth Division was rushed to Alamein from Syria in July 1942, Major Wheatley and the commanding officer of an infantry battalion were taken prisoners and flown to Italy. Major Wheatley later transferred to a prison camp at Sulmonia, where he spent twelve months before escaping.

When Italy finally collapsed in September last, a number of officers and men endeavoured to escape from their internment camp, and Major Wheatley, with a companion, managed to slip through the German cordon. After a trying and exciting six weeks hiding in and passing through enemy occupied territory, they eventually reached the British line.

On being repatriated to Australia, Major Wheatley landed at Melbourne early last week and arrived home on Wednesday. He is at present staying with his parents at Rossmore, and expects to shortly rejoin his old unit.[40]

Camden News Thursday 1 November 1945, page 4

News has been received that two of our local soldiers have died whilst Prisoners of War in Japanese hands: Pte. Jim Auld and Pte. Jack Clissold. As a tribute to their memory the flag at the Town Hall was flown half-mast.[41]

Camden News Thursday 8 November 1945, page 4

Honour Roll

The death is announced of five more local Prisoners of War: —

L/Sgt. Arthur Chapman, son of the late Mr. Joseph Chapman of Narellan, is reported to have died whilst a prisoner of war in Borneo in July last. Arthur was a brother of Mrs. A. E. Watson, Narellan; Mrs. F. King, of Albion Park ; Mrs. B. Vannan, Leichhardt ; and Mr. O. Chapman of Fairfield.

Colin Chapman, A.I.F., of The Oaks, died at Sandakan, Borneo, 4th June, 1945.

Sgt. Barrie Whitehead, A.I.F. late of the Bank of New South Wales, Camden, died at Borneo on 13th July, 1945.

Driver G. J. O'Loughlan, A.I.F., also of The Oaks, died at Sandakan, Borneo, 4th June, 1945.

Pte. A. J. Carneth, A.I.F., late of Narellan, died at Sandakan, Borneo on 5th June, 1945.

The army authorities have announced the death of Alfred Tritton, late of Camden and Commonwealth Bank at Rabaul. As a prisoner of war with the A.I.F., he was on board the Japanese vessel Montevideo which was torpedoed on 1st July, 1942, and then met his death. He was 34 years of age, and as an old Camden boy will be well remembered throughout the district.[42]

James William Boyd

Private NX49963

Enlisted:	Australian Army, 31 October 1941, Paddington, NSW
Unit:	2/20 Australian Infantry Battalion
Born:	4 March 1914 Melbourne, Vic
Parents:	James Boyd & Mary Dillon
Married:	Elsie May Chesham
Residence:	Camden, NSW
Next of Kin:	John Boyd
POW:	Prisoner of the Japanese
Died:	16 May 1945 Sandakan, Borneo; Prisoner of War; age: 31 years
Buried:	His body was never recovered, but his name is perpetuated on Panel 13 of the Memorial to the Missing, Labuan War Cemetery, Malaysia
Roll of Honour:	Camden, NSW
Note:	Died of malaria and beri-beri at Sandakan

Boyd, James William

AUSTRALIAN MILITARY FORCES

District Records Office
R.A.S. Showground Sydney
4 May 1942

Dear Madam,

I have been directed by the Minister for the Army to advise you that no definite information is at present available in regard to the whereabouts or circumstances of your husband, Number NX49963, Private James William Boyd, 2/20th Battalion A.I.F. and to convey to you the sincere sympathy of the Minister and the Military Board in your natural anxiety in the absence of news concerning him.

It is felt that you will readily appreciate, owing to the nature of the recent operations in the theatre of war in which he was engaged and the difficulties which have arisen in communicating with units which are located in territory now held by the enemy, that some time must necessarily elapse before further information becomes available.

Private Boyd 31 October 1941

You may rest assured, however, that the utmost endeavour will continue to be made through every possible source including the International Red Cross Society to obtain at the earliest moment a definite report which, when received, will be conveyed to you by telegram immediately. In the meantime it would be appreciated if you could forward full particulars to this office as quickly as possible of any information whatsoever you may receive from any other source, as it may be of the greatest value in supplementing or verifying the official investigations which are being made.

Yours faithfully,
H. G. Bennett Major
Officer in Charge of Records

NX49963
Pte James William Boyd
20 June 1942

My dearest wife,
I am a prisoner of war and I am in good health, and don't worry. Love to all.
James William Boyd

Dear Elsie,
Have received no letter yet.
My health is good.
Hope everything is well with you, and you are receiving your allotment.
Please remember me to all at home.
J.W. Boyd
P.O.W. Camp, Borneo

TELEGRAM 1 Army Records via Sydney 60/15/10 pm

Postal ACK. Delivery Personal
It is with deep regret that I have to inform you that NX49963 Pte James William Boyd died whilst prisoner of war at Sandakan Borneo on 17 May 1945 and desire to convey to you the profound sympathy of the Minister for the Army.

Minister for the Army

Arthur William Chapman

Corporal NX27779

Enlisted:	Australian Army 10 June 1940 Paddington, NSW
Unit:	2/20 Australian Infantry Battalion
Born:	20 February 1905 Narellan, NSW
Parents:	Joseph Chapman & Sevira Jane Brailsford
Occupation:	Carrier
Spouse:	Ruby May Fisher; Married: 1920 Armidale, NSW
Residence:	Leichhardt, NSW
Next of Kin:	Gloria Chapman
POW:	Prisoner of the Japanese
Died:	9 February 1945
Buried:	Labuan Memorial, Malaysia. Panel 13
Roll of Honour:	Camden, NSW
Note:	Captured 26 March 1942 in Borneo

Chapman, Arthur William

Camden News Thursday 6 March 1941, page 3

Letters From the Front

Mrs. A. E. Watson, Narellan, has word, undated, from her brother, Pte. Arthur Chapman: —

"On the ocean somewhere I do not know, and I do not know where we are going, but I suppose we will soon know, and I hope it shall not be long before we get a go at some of those war mongers. All the boys are anxiously waiting. We are on a liner bound for somewhere, and my word we are getting great meals and I have not been a bit sick so far. The water has been very calm, but today she is rocking and some of the other boys are sick. It would be a shame to get sick and not be able to eat the wonderful eats and drink the cheap beer — it is only 1/- for a dixie and they hold just on a quart; also the tobacco is only 1/- for 2 oz. tin. We have parades during the day, and go to bed about half past nine at night, but it is a great change from camp life. We have hot and cold water aboard, and hot and cold salt water baths. You cannot get a lather with the soap, but you can buy special salt water soap, so I am going to try it. I get a cup of tea in the morning for a few pence. How is Albert? I hope his arm is on the mend. Remember me to everybody."

[Letters from boys at the front are most interesting to their friends; pass the news on to them through "The Camden News."][43]

Neil Donaldson

Private NX7744

Enlisted:	Australian Army 7 November 1939 Paddington, NSW
Unit:	2/1 Battalion
Born:	16 February 1918 Sydney, NSW
Parents:	Alexander Henry Donaldson & Elsie I M Bruce
Residence:	Oakdale, NSW
Next of Kin:	E Hooper
Discharged:	20 September 1943
POW:	Prisoner of the Germans

Donaldson, Neil

Camden News Thursday 11 December 1941, page 5

PRISONER OF WAR
NEIL DONALDSON

The hon. secretary of the A.M.P. Society's Staff Comforts Fund, Sydney, is in receipt of a letter from Pte. Neil Donaldson, Prison of War, (formerly of the Boys' Home, Camden) written from Stalag XIII C, Deutschland, in which he refers to the Camden Women's Voluntary Services, Because of this the above Comforts Fund forwards to the Camden Women's Voluntary Services a copy of the letter which reads: —

"This letter will serve to explain why I have not acknowledged the receipt of any parcels from you lately. The authorities allow us to receive a parcel through the Red Cross of not more than eleven pounds in weight. Knowing how willingly you have been to help me with parcels I felt it would not be out of place to send you this card. The Camden Women's Voluntary Services has been good enough to help me and I wonder if you would be good enough to help me to inform them of the position in which I am placed, and if possible to send them a sample of this paper. Thanking you for past favours."

NEIL DONALDSON.[44]

Camden News Thursday 4 October 1945, page 4

Mr. Neal Donaldson, one of our local Servicemen, a returned Prisoner of War from Germany, is opening up business in Camden, having purchased the catering and refreshment rooms conducted by Mr. H. S. Kelloway. The transfer of the business to Mr. Donaldson takes place on 1st November.[45]

Harold Augustus, (Bill) Fallon

Driver QX18021

Enlisted:	Australian Army 1 August 1940 Warwick, Qld
Unit:	105 General Transport Company
Born:	4 December 1902, Camden, NSW
Parents:	Thomas Fallon & Ellen Devitt
Residence:	Warwick, Qld
Next of Kin:	Francis Fallon
Discharged:	26 November 1943
POW:	Prisoner of the Japanese
Died:	26 November 1943 Died of illness Burma
Buried:	Thanbyuzayat War Cemetery, Myanmar. A4.C.7
Roll of Honour:	Camden, NSW

Fallon, Harold Augustus (Bill)

Camden News Thursday 28 June 1945, page 4

DEATH OF PTE. BILL FALLON WHILE PRISONER OF WAR

Sad news has been received by Mr. Wes Fallon of Werombi, of the death of his brother, Pte. H. A. (Bill) Fallon, whilst Prisoner of War in Japan. The Army authorities wrote stating that information had been received from the International Red Cross Committee Geneva, that the Japanese authorities at Tokyo have reported by cable that Pte. H. A. Fallon died of illness whilst Prisoner of War in Thai Camp on 22nd November, 1943. Cause stated to be malaria.

Pte. Bill. Fallon enlisted from Camden and was with the A.I.F. in Malaya, where he was taken prisoner with his unit. He was the youngest son of the late Mr. Thos. Fallon of Werombi. There are four brothers, Messrs. Frank (Ryde), Wes (Werombi), Charlie (Ryde) and Mac (Melbourne), also two sisters, Mrs. Warren (Ryde) and Mrs Murdoch (Newcastle).[46]

Francis Orchard Gunn

Gunner NX28052

Enlisted:	Australian Army, 4 June 1940 Paddington, NSW
Unit:	2/15 Field Regiment
Born:	27 January 1914 Camden, NSW
Parents:	William George Gunn & Valerie Helena Jex
Occupation:	Orchard hand at Camden Park
Residence:	Camden Park, NSW
Next of Kin:	Valerie Gunn
POW:	Prisoner of the Japanese
Died:	16 September 1943 Died of illness Burma
Buried:	Thanbyuzayat War Cemetery, Burma (Myanmar)
Memorial:	Camden General Cemetery

Gunn, Francis Orchard

Camden News Thursday 17 August 1944, page 4

News was received in Camden last week that Gunner F. Orchard Gunn, son of Mrs. V. Gunn, and the late Mr. William Gunn, of Camden Park, died while a prisoner of war in Japan. The death was reported to have occurred on September 16 of last year.[47]

Eric George Kelloway
Private N243748 (NX73637)

Enlisted:	Australian Army 24 September 1941 Camden, NSW; Australian Army 3 December 1941 Paddington, NSW
Unit:	45 Battalion; 2/20 Battalion
Born:	24 February 1921 Camden, NSW
Parents:	Horace Stanley Kelloway & Minnie Price
Spouse:	Doreen Catherine Dennis; Married: In 1945 at Parramatta, NSW
Residence:	Camden, NSW
Next of Kin:	Horace Kelloway
Discharged:	18 December 1945
POW:	Prisoner of the Japanese
Died:	18 October 1996 Barrack Point, NSW

Kelloway, Eric George

CamdenNews Thursday 24 June 1943, page 2

Mr. and Mrs. H. S. Kelloway are in receipt of news from the Minister for the Army that their son, Eric, who has been posted as missing since the fall of Singapore, is now reported a Prisoner of War in an internment camp at Tokyo, Japan.[48]

Camden News Thursday 13 April 1944, page 2

Mr. and Mrs. H. S. Kelloway this week received a cheerful letter from their son, Eric, prisoner of war in a camp at Tokyo, Japan. Eric writes of being well, and conveys personal greetings to all at home. He had received a 2nd letter from his father and looks for an early reunion, but in the meantime he asked that his new niece be well looked after.[49]

Camden News Thursday 20 September 1945, page 1

Mr. and Mrs. H. S. Kelloway are in receipt of a cable from their son Eric, who has, since the fall of Singapore, been a prisoner of war. The message states he is well, at present in Manila, and will see you soon.[50]

Edwin Morton Rapley

Gunner NX26340

Enlisted:	Australian Army, 18 June 1940, Paddington, NSW
Unit:	2/15 Field Regiment
Born:	1 October 1910 at Camden, NSW
Parents:	William Rapley & Mary Jane Small
Spouse:	Leone Robert Hewett;
	Married: 29th September 1947 at Camden, NSW
Residence:	Camden, NSW
Next of Kin:	William Rapley
Discharged:	18 January 1946
POW:	Prisoner of the Japanese
Died:	29 September 1947 Razorback, NSW
Buried:	St. John's C/E Camden
Note:	Killed in MV accident

Rapley, Edwin Morton

Camden News Thursday 14 October 1943, page 2

Mr. J. Howe last night, Wednesday, on his short wave wireless, picked up Tokyo, Japan, in the Prisoners of War Session, when a message was read from Ted Rapley of Camden, to his sister, Miss Nita Rapley. His message was that he was well, and would appreciate parcels of comforts.[51]

Camden News Thursday 20 September 1945, page 2

Among the prisoners of war released in the Far East is Gunner E. M. Rapley; son of Mrs. Rapley of Menangle Rd., Camden.[52]

Camden News Thursday 11 October 1945, page 4

Camden to-day (Thursday) will welcome home another ex-Prisoner of War in the person of Mr. E. (Ted) Rapley, A.I.F., son of Mrs. Rapley, of Menangle Road.[53]

Charles Robertson (Bob) Skene

Lieutenant

Unit:	2nd Gurkha Regiment
Born:	26 May 1914 Assam, India
Parents:	Curtis Skene & Margaret (Meg) Jessop
Spouse:	Elizabeth Wheatley; Married: 1 July 1938 St. Mark's CofE North Audley Street, London, England
POW:	Prisoner of the Japanese; Changi

Skene, Charles Robertson (Bob)

Camden News Thursday 21 January 1943, page 4

Lieut. Bob Skene, Australian polo player, who has been missing since February, is a prisoner of war in Malaya. Mrs. Skene received the news a few days ago from the India Office. Bob joined the Indian Army in 1940, and was posted to the 2nd Gurkha Regiment which was in action against the Japanese from the time the Malay States were invaded until the fall of Singapore. From that day nothing was heard of him, and his country and sporting friends will be pleased to know he is safe. Mrs. Skene's brother, Major Max Wheatley, is in an Italian concentration camp near Rome. Letters to his family indicate that he is in good health.[54]

Norman Evan Segal

Signalman NX43572

Enlisted:	Australian Army, 25 August 1941, Wilton, NSW
Unit:	8 Corps of Signals
Born:	12 June 1922 Campbelltown, NSW
Parents:	Cyril Segal & Jessie Mary Percival
Spouse:	Phyllis May Smith ; Married: 1948 Parramatta, NSW
Residence:	Wilton, NSW
Next of Kin:	Cyril Segal
Discharged:	25 January 1946
POW:	Prisoner of the Japanese

Segal, Norman Evan

Camden News Thursday 25 May 1944, page 5

News From P.O.W.

Mr. E. A. Wintle, of Maylands, Western Australia, while listening to the Japanese-controlled radio station at Java, heard the announcer read the following message for Mr. Cyril Segal, Wilton, via Picton.

"From Signalman N. E. Segal, P.O.W. (959) Dear dad, sisters and brothers. Just a few lines to say I am in excellent spirits and good health. Hope all you are the same. Please send photos of each and all. Also ask Norma to send one of herself. Love to all, your loving son and brother, Norman."

Not having heard from Norman for six months, Mr. Segal naturally was pleased to receive the message. Norman has been a prisoner of war since March. 1941, and will be 21 on the 12th of June.[55]

Amos Richard Skinner

Private NX24832

Enlisted:	Australian Army, 3 June 1940, Paddington, NSW
Unit:	2/29 Battalion
Born:	21 February 1914 Camden, NSW
Parents:	Amos Roy Skinner & Maude Kathleen Stapleton
Residence:	Camden, NSW
Next of Kin:	Amos Skinner
Discharged:	20 December 1945
POW:	Prisoner of the Japanese
Died:	15 March 1997 Crows Nest, NSW

Skinner, Amos Richard

Camden News Thursday 27 September 1945, page 1

LETTER FROM TOKYO

Pte. Amos R. Skinner, released Prisoner of War, writing from Tokyo to his mother at Camden:— "You can't imagine how much you all have occupied my thoughts during the last 3½ years. I hope you are all as well as I am at present. I sent you a cable, and this morning a Petty Officer from an Australian warship came on board and got our names and addresses; he told us he would radio home. I might mention there are only five of us Australians on board a British ship at Yokohama. The British sailors are really marvellous; they cannot do enough for us. It was a great relief for us when the war ended on August 15. I cannot describe the Japanese. They are the most cruel, barbaric people I've ever been in contact with, and no punishment will be good enough for them. I was taken from Singapore to Burma in May 1943, and worked on the construction of the Monemein to Bangkok railway. We did it in two years, 20,000 men dying. When we finished that the Japs took a thousand of us to Saigon in Indo China, intending to take us to Japan. Anyhow they were unable to get us away, they worked us there for three months, and then took us right down through Thailand and Malaya by rail to Singapore. We stayed there six months and came to Japan in January this year. We have been working in coal mines. I might mention that Orchard Gunn was the only Camden chap with me in Burma and he died on 16th Sept., 1943."

Amos will arrive on British Escort Carrier H.M.S. Ruler in Sydney today. Also on the same boat is F/O A.M. Brown of Camden.[56]

Camden News Thursday 4 October 1945, page 4

The first released Prisoner of War from Japan to arrive in Camden is Pte. Amos Skinner, who returned home on Thursday last. Despite the appalling conditions under which he existed during the past three and a half years, Pte. Skinner has already felt the benefit of his freedom, and is at present enjoying 28 days leave renewing old acquaintances.[57]

Merchant Navy

The term Merchant Navy refers to commercial shipping and crews. During the Second World War Merchant Navy ships carrying valuable cargoes were at just as much risk as Royal Australian Navy (RAN) warships. They were attacked in distant waters and within sight of the Australian coastline while traversing much-frequented trade routes. However, the enemy's policy of unrestricted warfare meant that even ships from neutral nations were at risk of attack from enemy ships.

Several men with connections to Camden served in the merchant navy during the Second World War.

Henry Bernard (Barney) French

Able Seaman

Enlisted:	Merchant Navy 19 June 1939 Melbourne, Vic
Unit:	Merchant Navy Ship "SS Rona"
Born:	7 August 1922 Camden, NSW
Parents:	Henry Stewart French & Grace Elizabeth Stuart
Spouse:	Patricia Clare Smeal; Married: 1945 Bankstown, NSW
Residence:	Sydney, NSW
Discharged:	5 July 1945
Died:	10 January 2005 Bankstown, NSW

French, Henry Bernard (Barney)

Barney is better known for his exploits after the end of the war. He became Assistant Secretary of the New South Wales Branch of the Australian Workers' Union, and later became Federal President in 1970 and served until 1980. French was an active member of the Australian Labour Party in the Federal Electorate of Blaxland and the State Seat of Bankstown. He was Vice-President of the ALP for ten years and in 1973 was elected as a Labour member to the New South Wales Legislative Council. He was Government Whip from 1984 to 1988 and Opposition Whip from 1988 to 1989.

George Joseph Kent

Able Seaman

Enlisted:	Merchant Navy 14 May 1941 Melbourne, Vic
Unit:	Merchant Navy Ship MV Kooringa
Born:	1924 Camden, NSW
Residence:	Camberwell, Vic
Discharged:	18 July 1945
Died:	31 May 2003 Melbourne, Vic

Kent, George Joseph

Little is known of Kent other than what appears in the Nominal Roll.

As the Second World War started, the Scottish company, McIlwraith McEacharn Ltd, was operating ten ships which were deployed in the Australian Merchant Navy. The *Kooringa* was built in 1938 and operated on the Australian coast, serving as a troopship and a carrier for returning prisoners-of-war.

2/1/1941 Port Side view of the Australian Cargo Vessel SS Kooringa.

George Valentine Mundle

Fourth Engineer

Enlisted:	Merchant Navy, 23 August 1944 Sydney, NSW
Unit:	Merchant Navy Ship MV Ngakuta
Born:	1922 Sydney, NSW
Parents:	George Valentine Mundle & Ellen Agnes Carter
Spouse:	Joan Beatrice Macarthur; Married: 1945 Sydney, NSW
Residence:	Millers Point, NSW
Discharged:	21 July 1946
Died:	28 May 1974 Millers Point, NSW

Mundle, George Valentine

Little is known of Mundle other than what appears in the Nominal Roll. Janice did not include any further details for George Mundle and there are no obvious articles from the *Camden News*.

Mervyn Joseph Starr

Able Seaman 2nd Grade

Enlisted:	Merchant Navy, 31 August 1939 Sydney, NSW
Unit:	Merchant Navy Ship RMS Niagara
Born:	21 March 1907 Camden, NSW
Parents:	Joseph Henry Starr & Ainslie Plimsoll Watt
Spouse:	Dulcie May Hamilton ; Married: 1944 Tamworth, NSW
Residence:	North Sydney, NSW
Discharged:	19 June 1940
Died:	5 August 1984 Westmead, NSW

Starr, Mervyn Joseph

On 19 June 1940 *RMS Niagara* under the command of Captain William Martin had just left Auckland, New Zealand and was off Bream Head, Whangarei, when she struck a mine laid by the German auxiliary cruiser *Orion* and sank in 121 metres of water. No lives were lost.

> # Charles Kingsley Varlow
> ### Able Seaman
>
> | | |
> |---|---|
> | **Enlisted:** | Merchant Navy, 10 December 1941 Sydney, NSW |
> | **Unit:** | Merchant Ship Caledonian Salvor |
> | **Born:** | 31 July 1925 Dora Creek, NSW |
> | **Parents:** | William Henry Varlow & Ella Irene Cowie |
> | **Residence:** | Dee Why, NSW |
> | **Died:** | 25 November 2013 Cotton Tree, Qld |

Varlow, Charles Kingsley

The *Caledonian Salvor* was a salvage tug that had originally been allocated to the British for operation in Australian waters. After the war it was transferred to Australia. The tug was placed in service as *0368 (Caledonian Salvor)* and, assigned to the Commonwealth Salvage Board as a salvage and repair ship in New Guinea.

Camden News Thursday 20 March 1941, page 6

Letters from the Front
Extracts from a letter from an Officer of a merchant vessel forwarded by Miss [Sibella] Macarthur Onslow:

Crew is made up of eleven different nationalities. The ship is well found and comfortable in every way and the pay is very good, but I guess we earn it. We are not allowed to carry any armament — not even a shotgun — but have good defences — or rather protections, in the way of steel and concrete shelters and a conning-tower from which to direct operations when the going is hot.

Our Second Engineer is quite a famous person, Miss Drummond;[i] the only sea-going woman British Engineer, I believe. She was sent here by the Ministry, who couldn't get another engineer to take on the job. She, as well as the C/E, self and Sparks, are all ex-B.I. She was at one time 3/E[ii] of the Mulbera, and has also been on the Blue Funnel boats to Australia. She had a very good job on shore in London, but gave it up to come back to sea for the war and served at Dunkirk and everywhere nasty you can think of. She is the most courageous woman I ever saw. She seems to be without fear or nerves. Her inside must be composed of steel, wire and copper wire and catgut. She is very good at her job and has an uncanny power over the engines, for which I once thanked God. She gets from ½ to ¾ knot more out of the ship on the same fuel in her watch than any of the others. I once asked her how she did it and she said: "Oh, I just talk nicely to them. You can coax or lead engines to do what you want, you must never drive them." Which of course, is as clear as mud. If some of the others did a spot of driving we might be across this ruddy pond a bit quicker. Nearly three blinking weeks it is going to take. We had a hell of an attack on the second day out, more than 400 miles from land. A big 4-engined brute went for us for 35 minutes all his bombs and ammunition were exhausted and he must have felt the breeze about his petrol for we made him cover a few hundred miles in circles dodging after us.

---

[i] Victoria Alexandrina Drummond MBE (1894–1978), was the first woman marine engineer in Britain and first woman member of Institute of Marine Engineers. During World War II she served at sea as an engineering officer in the British Merchant Navy and received awards for bravery under enemy fire.
[ii] Third Engineer

We met each rush in the same way, by keeping on a steady course and letting him get almost into bombing position and then at the estimated time of release pushing the helm if possible, to swing the ship at the second when he pulled the release. The scheme was so successful that three times he couldn't get into bombing position at all and had to do another big circle round. All were most damnably close and the noise and concussion hellish as the guns (he had two in two turrets, ahead and astern) kept going till near the end, when apparently they were out of ammunition, or seized up with heat.

Everything breakable in the ship is in smithereens. We have only a few cups and have to eat all off one plate at meals. All the phones and speaking-tubes were put out of action, and clocks, electric light, etc., but she still floats and only makes a little water which the pumps keep under. We had the joy of hearing on the Italian radio that night of our destruction by a German bomber — for the second time in three weeks, as before I joined the ship 'Haw Haw' announced she had been sunk in Portlands Road during the mass attack there (three bombs were aimed at her but missed).

When it was all over and the black abomination had disappeared to the Eastward, I for one, felt dazed — it was like a miracle. There was the same lovely cloudless sky and summer blue sea. The ship was still plunging along to the Westward. Only the shattered boats and the decks, rooms and saloon littered with spent bullets, splinters and rubbish showed that something had been doing. Besides Almighty God we have to thank the coolness and the skill of the Captain, who had to judge every order in terms of seconds and never once made a mistake; but perhaps, even more, that very noble lady the 2/E.[i] She took charge and in ten minutes she had "talked" to those engines to such good purpose that our miserable speed of 9 knots had risen to 12½ and was still going up when she eased down at "All Clear." That speed had never before been recorded in all her eighteen years. It is only in the last few days that I have heard what happened down below in that ghastly half hour. She was talking to the C/E[ii] and me on deck in her Sunday best uniform after breakfast, when the alarm gong went. She went at once and took charge down below. After the first salvo, which flung her against the levers and nearly stunned her, she realised that there was little hope. She told the other engineers to open up the fuel injectors and to start others, and began operating the main steam injectors (throttle) bit by bit. Then calling the engine room and stokehold staff she gave them the last order — pointing with her long arm to the ladder — "get out." So she gave them a chance for their lives and stayed there alone, where she knew she had none. It must have been pure Hell down there. Two cast iron pipes were fractured, electric wires parted, tubes broken and joints started, but her iron body and mighty heart stood it. The main injection pipe just above her head started a joint and scalding steam whizzed past her head. With anyone less skilled down there that pipe would have burst under the extra pressure, but she nursed it through each explosion of each salvo, easing down when she judged from the nearness of the plane's engines that the bombs were about to fall, holding on for all she was worth to a stanchion as they burst and then opening up the steam again. If the pipe had gone we would have stopped and it would have been all UP. By getting the speed it gave the helm a chance to move the clumsy hulk, which it wouldn't have had at less speed, and literally every second mattered in the swing. I saw her once during the action when I had to dodge along to the W.T. room and looked down the skylight, hoping to be able to shout a few words to cheer her. She was standing on the control platform, one long arm stretched about her head and her hand holding down the spoke of the throttle control as if trying by her touch to urge another pound of steam through the straining pipe. Her face, as expressionless as the bulkhead behind her and as ghastly white in colour, was turned towards the sunlight, but she did not see me. From the top of her forehead, down her long face, completely closing one eye, trickled a wide black streak of fuel Oil from a strained joint. That alone must have been agony. She had jammed

---

[i] Second Engineer
[ii] Chief Engineer

her ears at first with oily waste to deaden the concussion and then, in a panic, tore it out again for fear she would not hear some vital order from the bridge — not knowing that all connection with the bridge was cut. She was about all in at the end, but within an hour was full of beans and larking about picking-up spent bullets and splinters. All round her, by the way, the platform was littered with bullets that came down from the skylight. They still sweep some up every day.

                          Cheer-oh.[58]

War's End

Camden News Thursday 24 October 1946, page 5

THE AFTERMATH OF WAR

From the war-wrecked lands overseas, comes a cry of utter despair,
For millions of folk are dying, of hunger and cold over there;
In sunny Australia to-day, we have strife and strikes of our own,
But the lack of food and clothing, to us in this land is unknown.

Wealth is a great power to-day, when used to help others in need,
But oft proves a curse to those men, who hoard it in prisons of greed,
I have seen strong men lose their lives, in a search for the Goddess Wealth,
Who has robbed them each day and night, of the precious blessing of health?

We may not have Wealth to help them, and yet each and all do our share,
By an inspection of wardrobes, and giving of clothes we can spare.
Think of the Children over there, perishing with hunger and cold,
While yours are so cosy and warm, 'neath covers which round them unfold.

Our Master loved little children, and gathered them into His arms,
And said to the crowd around Him, in that voice which hath many charms,
In-as-much as ye have done this, to the least of these that I love,
I will certainly reward you in that Heavenly Home above . . . .

—*HORACE DOUST, Camden* [59]

Welcome Home

Camden News Thursday 4 October 1945, page 1

THANKSGIVING

The boys are coming back. From the battlefields of the Pacific, from Japanese horror camps, Nazi stalags, they're flowing, in a steady, increasing stream, back to the soil for which they have fought and suffered.

They have finished their job. But if Australia is really to be the "land fit for heroes" we promised when they went away, we haven't finished our task.

A heavy duty rests upon all of us to see that nothing stands in the way of the full rehabilitation of every man and woman who was prepared to offer up youth, and even life itself, to preserve a way of life we called ours.

Until every prisoner of war has been repatriated, every one of the hundreds of thousands in the services re-established adequately in civilian life, and thorough provision made for maintaining those forces we may contribute to aid in the occupation of enemy territory — until then, we Australians will not be able to feel that we have honourably discharged our obligations.

The trumpets and the drums of war may have ceased to sound, but our readiness to shoulder our responsibilities as citizens of a victorious nation must be no less real than it was in the days when our fate was still in the balance.

For a lost peace means a lost war. Failure to play our individual roles in laying the foundations of a prosperous post-war Australia, will be treachery to our fighting men no less real than would have been our betrayal of them to the enemy.

War is a costly business. But so is the transition to peace. We were prepared to lend until it hurt to wage a war to keep the enemy from desecrating our homes. We must be prepared to lend as freely so that those who kept the enemy from our shores may have homes, and jobs, and the peace of mind they have so richly earned.

Have you ever thought of the large sums that will be necessary to care, for an indefinite period in some cases, for our sick and wounded? Have you ever thought of the cost of maintaining our service personnel until they can find a place for themselves in civilian life? Have you considered just how much governments will need to provide for the professional and technical education of young men and women who spent, in the service of the nation, the years which they would normally have devoted to preparing themselves for a career or a trade?

All these things have to be done. The money for them must be forth coming. And it is our job — our privilege — to help in the task of providing it.

It is not a question of whether each one of us is to co-operate in, making the Fourth Victory Loan a success. We are, we must!

No, our only decision is how much we are going to set aside out of our savings or our earnings for this purpose. Whatever the sum may be, it must be the maximum.

For it should be our proud determination to make the Victory Loan a Thanksgiving Loan, a tangible demonstration of our gratitude for victory, of our deep thankfulness for the return of our children, our husbands and our lovers, and of our undying gratitude to our dead.

Not one of us would want to be out of a national gesture of such high significance; and not one of us shall be.

As citizens, we have helped make every past war loan a success. Let us make the Fourth Victory Loan — the Thanksgiving Loan — such a magnificent success that it will stand as a monument to victory and to our determination to make that victory worthwhile.[60]

Camden News Thursday 24 February 1944, page 5

SOLDIERS' WELCOME.
(By R.S.L. Publicity Officer)

Without a doubt, the decision to welcome home the Servicemen discharged, or on leave from battle areas, as conducted last Friday by Camden Old Diggers as a tribute by them to the prowess of the New Digger, was a happy one judging by the splendid co-operation of everyone concerned — just as it should be.

Upwards of forty attended by the Old Diggers' invitation to honour the ten young warriors, looking fit and well, and who were Sgt. J. N. Dunk (served Middle East); S/Sgt. T. N. Filby (M.E. and New Guinea); Dvr. J. Holdsworth (Papua); Sgt. Hall (M.E., N.G. and Goodenough Island); L/Bdr. R. L. Hughes (Torres Str.); Dvr. M. Lillis (Torres Str.); Dvr. R. C. Lindsay (Papua); Pte. V. N. Rapley (Nth. Aust.); Pte. L. R. Marden (N.G.); and Pte. A. Reynolds (N.A.)

After the Loyal Toast, the R.S.L. President, Mr. E. H. K. Downes, extended a hearty welcome home to the lads in the most sincere terms, with the assurance that the R.S.L. Camden was inspired to keep the flag up right high for the benefit of our fighters now and on their return. On the President calling upon the Mayor to support him, Alderman Kelloway expressed his great pleasure at the invitation and he wished the guests to know his remarks represented his fellow aldermen and the general public. Mr. Kelloway urged the boys and their comrades to take up civil responsibilities when peace comes, just as they have accepted their war-time ones. (Such has always been one of the R.S.L's aims. Mr. Mayor!)

The toast to their health was responded to by S/Sgt. Filby and Dvr. Lindsay - the other eight should be wonderful jungle fighters - so quiet under fire, but well in position to advance on their good objectives later on when such verbal barrage lifted.

With musical honours, V/P de Saxe thanked the C.W.A. Younger Set for assisting so well and fully in the evening at short notice, to which Mrs. Sparks, their President, responded very nicely; to the Red Cross to whom he paid full tribute, and fittingly replied to by Mrs. E. H. K. Downes in the apologised-for absence of the President, Mrs. R. E. Jefferis, and to Camden W.V.S., Mr. de Saxe gave praise for comforts so regularly sent. (Bill even went so far as to forgive her when she got his meals late on packing days). Their President, Mrs. Crookston, in acknowledgment, said it was a labour of love and, later she spoke with each of the boys as to their parcels.

The success of the evening was due quite a lot to Mrs. Ray Martin of Sydney, whose man is soldiering on in a battle area, and she is doing her bit by entertaining the troops regularly at the Anzac Buffet, Camps, and over the air. Mrs. Martin kept our dance music going, entertained with song, and generally made it easier for Mr. Treasurer Donnelley, the M.C., who did a fine job in the Donnelley style. (Frank, your tailor is a beaut, or have you the perfect form?) V/P Stibbard was given the pleasure of thanking these two artists. General regret was expressed at the absence on holidays of Secretary F. Coates.

Camden R.S.L. President and Diggers are most thankful to all those who contributed in any way to the pleasure given those Ten Warriors, and it is greatly regretted that illness and other causes prevented more of those on leave and discharged, from being present. [61]

Camden News Thursday 20 September 1945, page 1

THESE AGONISING WEEKS

For countless Australian families the past fortnight has imposed the greatest emotional stress of the six years of war.

It has been a period of tense anxiety, of abounding relief, and of bitter sorrow, in accordance with the news received from prison camps in Japanese hands - or the absence of news.

With those in our midst who have been advised of the safety of kinsfolk, lost to the world for agonising years, the community rejoices. It looks forward to the day of actual home-coming, and hopes that in the meantime the miracle-working processes of nature will have repaired much of the physical hurt which long and cruel incarceration inflicted.

For those whose word is that their loved ones have made the last supreme sacrifice, and for those still in suspense regarding the fate of their men-folk, there will be sympathy, sincere and profound. Beyond all our superficial differences of creed and politics and what not, we are all limited in the basic instincts of our common humanity. We rejoice and we suffer together; we are sharers in the ultimate, fundamental things of our life.

The revelations which have come from the prison camps cannot do other than fill the world with horror. They show the suave, so courteous Jap. in his true colours as a sadistic fiend - a barbaric survival but thinly veiled with a veneer of civilisation. The dominant thought in the mind of Australians must be a sense of profound thankfulness that our country was snatched from the invader. In the light of what we now know, of the mental attitude of the Nipponese toward members of the white race within their power, it is not difficult to conjecture what would have been our fate under Japan's Eastern Co-prosperity Sphere. For such a deliverance, and for those who in their own bodies made it possible, the people of this country must retain perpetual gratitude.

Over and beyond all immediate consideration, however, must be the determination that never again will the nations resort to war and mutual destruction for the settlement of their national differences. This, surely, is the war to end war, and even though primitive instincts in human nature impel to revenge, a realisation of the results which must inevitably follow another world war must temper all resort to physical force.

It is providential that the annihilating power of atomic energy, releasing forces beyond anything hitherto conceived in the mind of men, should have been revealed before the present conflict ended. We now know what can be done when primeval force is turned to destructive ends, the lesson of it should make the war-worker tremble before invoking once again the arbitrariness of war.

Meantime, the thoughts of the community are with those in our midst who have endured the long years of waiting for news regarding the fate of those of their home circles who fell into enemy hands.

With the termination of the war the Voluntary Air Observer Corps is disbanding. The observation post on Macarthur Park closes down today, Thursday, and it is expected the post will be cleared by Saturday.[62]

Eric George Kelloway (See page 69)

Camden News Thursday 11 October 1945, page 1

WELCOME HOME

The returned Prisoner of War, Eric Kelloway, son of the Mayor and Mayoress of Camden, Mr. and Mrs. H. S. Kelloway, was enthusiastically welcomed home on Tuesday. A number of friends gathered together to express a welcome that was spontaneous. Sergt K. C. Alder, who had been a Prisoner of War in Japanese hands for over three years, also returned the same evening, and joined his wife and family residing in Hill St., Camden.[63]

Edwin Morton Rapley (See page 70)

Camden News Thursday 11 October 1945, page 4

Camden to-day (Thursday) will welcome home another ex-Prisoner of War in the person of Mr. E. (Ted) Rapley, A.I.F., son of Mrs. Rapley, of Menangle Road.[64]

Keith McKnight DFC

Flying Officer 421612

Enlisted:	Royal Australian Air Force, 28 February 1942, Sydney, NSW
Unit:	1668 Communications Unit
Born:	5 August 1922 Menangle, NSW
Parents:	Alexander Andrew McKnight & Mary Matilda McPherson
Occupation:	Salesman
Spouse:	Hazel Gwyneth Howe; Married: 1947 Canterbury, NSW
Next of Kin:	Alec McKnight
Discharged:	29 September 1945
Died:	20 December 1989 Menangle, NSW
Buried:	St. James' C/E Menangle columbarium
Honours:	Distinguished Flying Cross

McKnight, Keith

Camden News Thursday 1 February 1945, page 2

Distinguished Flying Cross.

Official announcement has been made of the Distinguished Flying Cross being awarded to Pilot Officer Keith McKnight of Camden. The award is for gallant service in action over enemy territory in Europe. Congratulations are extended to Keith and his parents, Mr. and Mrs. A. McKnight of Alpha Rd, Camden.[65]

Camden News Thursday 8 November 1945, page 1

R.S.S. & A.I.L.A.
CAMDEN SUB-BRANCH NOTES.
(By Publicity Officer).

Our October meeting was again well attended, when further nice plans of our memorial club building were discussed. New member, Keith McKnight, whose piloting of Lancasters and Halifaxs brought him a worthy D.F.C., was welcomed by President Edgar Downes.[66]

Lyle Doust

Warrant Officer 420161

Enlisted:	Royal Australian Air Force 11 October 1941 Sydney, NSW
Unit:	466 Squadron (UK)
Born:	11 December 1920 Camden, NSW
Parents:	Albert Doust & Annie Dorothy Wheeler
Spouse:	Marjorie Joan Willi; Married: On 17th April 1946 Yass, NSW
Residence:	Yass, NSW
Next of Kin:	Albert Doust
Discharged:	16 October 1945
POW:	Prisoner of Germany
Died:	21 February 2005 Canberra, ACT

Doust, Lyle

Camden News Thursday 2 August 1945, page 4

Camden welcomed home on Saturday last, two of its Servicemen who had been away for some time actively engaged overseas.

F/O Keith McKnight D.F.C., son of Mr. Alex McKnight, Alpha Road, Camden, after 2½ years with the R.A.A.F in England, taking part in no less than 39 operational flights over Germany, is now on five weeks leave.

W/O Lyle Doust, R.A.A.F. navigator, son of Mr. and Mrs. Bert Doust of Yass, formerly of Camden, was also among those repatriated home. Lyle was for a year and five months a Prisoner of War in Germany, first at Stalag III, and then when the Russians entered Poland, was transferred to the prison camp at Stalag IV, then as the Allies progressed he was on forced marches from 6th February to 4th May, being liberated a few days before VE Day. Lyle has two brothers on Active Service, W/O Rodney Doust, with the R.A.F. in India, and Kevin Doust, with the A.I.F. in New Guinea.[67]

Ivor Morgan Evans

Signalman/Warrant Officer 424399 (N218620)

Enlisted:	Royal Australian Air Force 23 December 1941 Sydney; Royal Australian Air Force 12 September 1942 Sydney
Unit:	1 Australian Motor Division Signals; 436 (RCAF) SQDN
Born:	30 July 1923 Singleton, NSW
Parents:	Ivor Evans & Nettie Blanch
Spouse:	Miriam Myrena Johnson; Married: 1949 Campbelltown, NSW
Residence:	Bondi, NSW
Next of Kin:	Christmas Evans
Discharged:	18 December 1946
Died:	27 August 1990 Ashfield, NSW

Evans, Ivor Morgan

Camden News Thursday 11 October 1945, page 4

Mr. and Mrs, C. Evans, Broughton St. Camden, have received word that their son, Wr/O. Ivor Evans, who has been with the RA.A.F. in Burma, is expected to arrive home on Monday next from India.[68]

Camden News Thursday 1 November 1945, page 4

W/O. Ivor Evans, son of Alderman and Mrs. C. Evans of Broughton Street, Camden, arrived home from service abroad on Sunday last. Warrant Officer Evans has had three years in the R.A.A.F. and was attached to the R.A.F. in India, and the Royal Canadian Air Force in Burma, where he participated in 800 hours in operational flights.[69]

Kenneth Scott Pratt

Private NX60527

Enlisted:	Australian Army 23 July 1940 Goulburn, NSW
Unit:	2/17 Australian Infantry Battalion
Born:	14 August 1916 Carcoar, NSW
Parents:	Matthew Thomas Pratt & Mary Gertrude Scott
Occupation:	Railway Porter
Spouse:	Lola Guy; Married: 1949 Burwood, NSW
Residence:	Cooma, NSW
Next of Kin:	Mathew Pratt
Discharged:	15 November 1945
Died:	9 May 2006 Albion Park, NSW

Pratt, Kenneth Scott

Camden News Thursday 15 November 1945, page 1

MENANGLE NEWS

After five years and four months in the A.I.F. Pte. Ken Pratt, second son of Mr. and Mrs. Pratt of Menangle Railway Station, arrived home recently from the Pacific war zone.

Prior to enlisting Ken was on the staff of Cooma Railway Station, but it was not long after the outbreak of war that he answered the call to arms and after undergoing the usual training was sent to the Middle East with the 9th Division. During his two years of service over there he qualified for the title of "Tobruk Rat" by spending 8 months in the historic defence of the now famous fort. On his return to Australia his unit was sent to New Guinea where during his eleven months there he took part in some very heavy engagements with, the enemy. Following New Guinea he was drafted to Borneo where the final 9 months of his service was spent. Although he took part in some of the hottest fighting of the war, it is good to know he came through unscathed and arrived home fit and well and is now looking forward to once again wearing civvies and enjoying a more peaceful existence and a cooler climate, after experiencing the heat of the African desert and the tropics north of Australia.[70]

Jean Kinnear Pratt

Teleprinter Operator WR/870

Enlisted:	WRAN 3 March 1943 Sydney, NSW
Unit:	HMAS Rushcutter
Born:	2 July 1918 Carcoar, NSW
Parents:	Matthew Thomas Pratt & Mary Gertrude Scott
Spouse:	Karl Erhard Timmel; Married: 1957 Campbelltown, NSW
Next of Kin:	Mary Pratt
Discharged:	19 November 1945
Died:	23 May 1979 Canberra, ACT

Pratt, Jean Kinnear

Camden News Thursday 15 November 1945, page 1

MENANGLE NEWS

It is also pleasing to know that W.R.A.N. Pte. Jean Pratt is now convalescing at home after a 9 months sojourn in No. 113 A.G.H. following a serious illness contracted whilst at Townsville early this year. This young lady joined the W.R.A.N.S some two years ago and saw service at several N.S.W. stations before going to Queensland. There are still two members of the Pratt family away on service (Fred and Robert) both being still somewhere amongst the islands up north.[71]

John David Pratt

Flight Sergeant 432727

Enlisted:	Royal Australian Air Force 29 January 1943 Sydney NSW
Unit:	1 Advanced Flying Unit
Born:	12 December 1924 Cowra, NSW
Parents:	Matthew Thomas Pratt & Mary Gertrude Scott
Occupation:	Audit Clerk
Residence:	Menangle, NSW
Next of Kin:	Matthew Pratt
Died:	Aircraft accident Cronk Ne Voddy Isle of Man 13 November 1944
Buried:	Jurby Churchyard isle of Man 11am Friday 17 November 1944
Roll of Honour:	Menangle, NSW
Note:	Aircraft Anson AX117 in flight from sea struck high ground, all crew killed; NAA: A705, 166/33/249

Pratt, John

Camden News Thursday 13 June 1946, page 2

MENANGLE NEWS
WELCOME HOME

To the accompaniment of heavy rain on the roof of the School of Arts Hall, Menangle held its welcome home to returned servicemen and women on Wednesday last, 5th June.

In spite of it being a very cold and wet night there was a splendid roll up to do honour to the guests of the evening. Had it been fine it is safe to say the building would scarcely have held all who would have attended.

The hall had been prepared for the occasion and looked gay with its decorations of flags, bunting, and greenery.

Proceedings opened with the singing of the National Anthem followed by all standing in silence in memory of those who would not return and with special regard to John Pratt who lost his life in an aircrash whilst with the R.A.A.F. in England.

The chairman announced that apologies had been received from several invited guests who were unable to be present, also from Colonel Edward Macarthur Onslow who was to have made the presentations of certificates on behalf of the people of Menangle, but who unfortunately had been at the last minute prevented from doing so by a business engagement. However Mr. Jeff Bate, M.L.A., and Rev. A. H. Kirk were present and would carry out that important duty.

First a nicely framed next-of-kin certificate was presented to Mr. and Mrs. Pratt by the Rev. Kirk, who in asking them to accept this token of appreciation said that whilst we all felt for them in their loss we also are proud and honoured to remember their son and to show in some small way appreciation of the sacrifice he made.

Mr. Jeff Bate then presented framed illuminated certificates, together with an envelope containing five £1 war saving certificates to each of the following or their representatives: — Miss M. W. Hickey and Miss Joan Pratt of the A.W.A.S. and Miss Jean Pratt of the

W.R.A.N.S.; Messrs. S. M. Bennett, G. H. Bunt, H. C. Bunt, H. K. Crisp, S.I Cook, J. A. Cummins, C. A. Dempsey, C. W. Evans, J. P. Goonan, G. Heighington, K. L. Hunt, E. S. Heighington, F. Heffernan, A. R. Lang, G. F. Martin, L. T. McGrath, K. S. Pratt, R. G. Pratt, B. M. Pratt and D. Pry.

In making the presentation Mr. Bate congratulated the men on their action in answering the call to arms, and said he was proud to have the privilege of welcoming them back to civil life and he hoped they would all find happiness and contentment, although at first it may be hard to settle down to the routine of everyday life after moving about so much.

After a message of good cheer and sincere wishes for her early restoration to good health had been forwarded to Miss Jean Pratt (who is at present in No. 11th A.G.H.) per medium of her parents, a vote of thanks to Rev. Kirk and Mr. Bate was proposed by Mr. T. Brown and was carried by acclamation.

Following this part of the programme, refreshments were served and the coffee and splendid assortment of eatables were much appreciated and enjoyed on such a cold evening. When everyone had done justice to the good things offering, the floor was prepared for dancing and the remainder of the evening was given over to that popular pastime. During the intervals Misses Ingleton and Rapley entertained with songs with banjo accompaniment and Mr. Ingleton also rendered songs whilst Mr. R. Watson conducted community singing. Mrs. Ingleton's orchestra from Picton provided the music for dancing and thereby fulfilled a wish expressed many months ago that they be allowed to give their services gratis for the occasion whenever it might be held.

Altogether the function was a splendid success, and in no small way was this success due to the secretary, Mr. N. Curry, who in addition to carrying out the work required by his position of secretary for the months of organising for the function, crowned it all by facing the elements in a nightmare drive to Picton for the orchestra when their transport arrangements failed at the eleventh hour, and again by making another trip to take them home after the function ended.[72]

Marjorie Wanda Hickey

Corporal NF445497

Enlisted:	Australian Army 15 December 1942 Paddington, NSW
Unit:	Australian Women's Army Service
Born:	16 December 1909 Sydney, NSW
Parents:	James Hickey & Wanda Zglinicki
Residence:	Menangle, NSW
Next of Kin:	James Hickey
Discharged:	21 November 1945

Hickey, Marjorie Wanda

There is only one reference to Miss Marjorie Hickey in the *Camden News*, and it was before the war.

Camden News Thursday 18 March 1937, page 5

Mr. James Hickey and his daughter, Miss Marjory Hickey, had a narrow escape from serious injury on Sunday afternoon last, whilst driving to Campbelltown. As they were passing through the railway viaduct at North Menangle a lorry travelling in the opposite direction crashed into their horse. Both occupants and the sulky were thrown to the roadway, but fortunately they escaped with a severe shaking. The horse was so badly injured that it died shortly afterwards, and the sulky and harness were considerably damaged. Several accidents have occurred at this dangerous spot, and a fatality is likely to occur unless something is done to alter the present conditions.[73]

Editors' comments

Janice left a manuscript consisted of a series of chapter headings grouping articles from the *Camden News* about people serving in World War II. Janice placed a panel summarising the person's life and service history at the front of each group.

Some of the connecting text and panel content was incomplete. There was no front matter, and much of the back matter was unfinished.

Janice's selection of material reflected Janice's interests and perspectives.

The Camden Historical Society added the front matter (title page, copyright page, dedication, table of contents, list of illustrations and introduction) and the back matter (appendix, bibliography, references, and index).

Janice's selection of people and articles was primarily left unchanged. If Janice had finished her book, she may have added other servicemen and woman from the district.

The Society did verify panel content against the defence and war service records from the National Archives of Australia (when available), the Australian War Memorial's Roll of Honour, the Australian Government Department of Veteran's Affairs Nominal Roll, and the Camden Remembers website. Most of the information was correct. Inconsistences were resolved by applying the references in the order listed.

Details of each quotation from the *Camden News* and other places are linked by an endnote number at the end of the quote to a line in the Bibliography. The quotations are reproduced as printed and so reflect language and punctuation conventions of their time and may seem unusual.

A list of the most common abbreviations used in World War II services records is published by the National Archives of Australia.[i]

Janice's panels sometimes contain marriage details after people's period of service. The source of this information is unclear and was not verified.

The residence in the panel is the place of residence at the time of enlistment.

The unit in the panel is generally the unit at the time of discharge. If a person was discharged from a hospital or equivalent, the unit is where the person last saw active service.

Readers who wish to suggest corrections should send the details to the secretary, Camden Historical Society, PO Box 566 Camden NSW 2570 Australia (secretary@camdenhistory.org.au).

The Society is pleased to publish the book as Janice wished and thanks Fletcher Joss from Egarag Pty Ltd for his great contribution in taking Janice's unfinished manuscript to publication.

---

[i] "Abbreviations used in World War I and World War II service records", accessed July 20, 2021, https://www.naa.gov.au/explore-collection/defence-and-war-service-records/researching-war-service/abbreviations-used-world-war-i-and-world-war-ii-service-records

Index

The index is divided into six groups: Awards, Diseases, Other, People, Places and Units. All are arranged in alphabetic order.

Awards

Air Force Cross (AFC), 9
Distinguished Flying Cross (DFC), 9, 88, 89
MBE, 80
Mentioned in Dispatches, 32
Order of Australia Medal (OAM), 53
Victoria Cross (VC), 11, 122

Diseases

Beri-beri, 63
Malaria, 20, 21, 39, 63, 67
Typhus, 39, 40

Other

Australian Comforts Fund, 18, 36, 66
BHP steelworks, 48
Camden Historical Society, 22
Camden Show Society, 53
Church of England, 50
Eastern Co-prosperity Sphere, 87
Elderslie Cricket Club, 41
Equator, 17
Free Masonry, 50
Glenmount Theatre, 20
Grimson & Ollis' orchestra, 26
International Date Line, 17
J-V Day, 54
Kelloway, Mrs. Kelloway's orchestra, 1, 87
Lutheran Church, 50
Methodist Church, 50
Monte Carlo Rally, 51
Presbyterian, 50
Roll of Honour, 25, 41
Rossmore Comforts Fund, 36
Royal Aero Club, 51
Soldiers & Citizens Association, 4
St. Paul, 49
Sydney Harbour Bridge, 48
V-J Day, 54
Voluntary Aid Detachment, 43
War Bonds, 12
Williams, Major, 32

People

Adams, Pte. H. S., 4
Adams, Signalman C. T., 4
Aiken, Captain Bill, 34, 35
Alder, Sergt K. C., 87
Anderson, Cr (Nepean Shire), 12, 13
Angilley, W, 24
Atfield, Donald Albert (Don), 4, 39
Attlee, Mr, 54
Auld, R. J., 4, 62
Barnes, Hannah Frances, 30
Bate
    Dame Zara, 5
    Gerta, 5, 6
    Henry Jefferson Percival, 5, 6, 93, 94
    Lily, 5
    Thelma, 5
Bates, Wing Commander, 3
Beckley, Rene, 56
Bennett
    A. L., 49
    Major H. G., 64
    S. M., 94
Biddle, Pte. R. J., 2
Bingham, Mr, 19
Blanch, Nettie, 90
Boehme, Jacob, 49
Bond
    Charlotte Elizabeth, 39
    J., 40
    James Adam, 39
Booth
    Alfred Joseph Lashma, 40, 62
    Charlotte Elizabeth, 39
    Edward James, 4, 39, 40
    Harold, 40
    Harry, 39
    Henrietta Matilda, 39
    Henry Robert, 39
    Miss Hilda, 40
Boyd
    Elsie May, 63
    James, 63
    James William, 64

Index

Brailsford
    James William, 63, 64
    Mary, 63
Brailsford
    Severia Jane, 65
Brew
    Mrs. J., 23
    Pte. Ron, 23
Brien, Michael, 1
Brown, F/O A.M., 73
Brown, Mr. T., 94
Bruce
    Elsie I. M., 66
    Pte. K. A., 2
Bunt
    Mr. G. H., 94
    Mr. H. C., 94
Cannan, Miss, 24
Carling
    Francis, 41
    Margaret Henrietta, 41
    Mr. and Mrs. J. S., 41
Carneth, Pte. A. J., 62
Carter, Ellen Agnes, 78
Carvith, A.J., 59
Chapman
    Arthur William, 65
    Colin, 59, 62
    Gloria, 65
    Joseph, 62, 65
    L/Sgt. Arthur, 62
    Mr. O., 62
    Ruby May, 65
    Severia Jane, 65
    W., 59
Chesham
    Elsie May, 63
    Harold Charles (Dick), 42
    John, 42
    Pte. Ron, 3
    Sarah Elizabeth, 42
Chisholm
    Sylvia Seton, 51
Churchill, Winston, 2, 37, 38
Clark
    David, 9
    Ivy Eileen, 9
    Leo, 59
    Mr. D., 9
    Squadron Leader James, 9
Clink, Cr (Nepean Shire), 13
Clissold, Pte. Jack, 62
Clowes
    Miss Elaine, 23
    Mr J., 23
Coates, Mr F., 86
Cole, Lucia (Lucy) Anne Daley, 44
Colleen, Cpl, 3
Collins, S.M., 49
Cook, Mr. S. I., 94
Cowle, Capt. F. E., 30
Cowrie, Ella Irene, 80
Crane, Gnr. R. W., 4
Crisp, Mr. H. K., 94
Crookston
    Dr. and Mrs., 43
    Dr. R. M., 2, 32, 43
    Jacqueline, 43
    Mrs., 86
    R, 43
    Suzanne Jean, 32, 34
Cross, Mrs, 19
Cruikshank, W. S., 1, 3
Cummins, Mr. J. A., 94
Curry, Mr. N., 94
Curtin, John, 37, 38
Davis
    Edward Allen, 28
    Frederick, 28
    Harriette Olive, 28
    Sarah Annie, 28
    William Benjamin, 28
Dawson, Sergeant Thomas Myles, 51
de Saxe, Mr., 86
Dempsey, Mr. C. A., 94
Dengate
    Colin, 59
    Mr. and Mrs. E. J., 59
Dennis, Doreen Catherine, 69
Devitt, Ellen, 67
Dickins, Dame Zara, 5
Dillon, Mary, 63
Dobell, William (artist), 57
Donaldson
    Alexander Henry, 66
    Elsie I M, 66
    Neil, 66
Donnelley, Mr. Treasurer, 86
Doust
    Albert, 89
    Annie Dorothy, 89
    Kevin, 89
    Lyle, 89
    Marjorie Joan, 89
    Mr. and Mrs. Bert, 89
    W/O Rodney, 89

Index

Downes
- Cr (Nepean Shire), 13, 86, 88
- Mr. and Mrs. R. F. A., 10
- Rupert Frederick Arding, 10
- Sgt. Pilot Rupert Frederick Arding (Derick), 10

Drew, Betty, 56
Drummond MBE, Miss Victoria Alexandrina, 80
Dunbar
- Mr. Wal, 24
- Pte. J. K., 4

Dundas, Douglas (artist), 57
Dunk
- Gnr. J. N., 3
- Sgt. J. N., 86

Edgar, Florence, 23
Edmondson
- John Hurst, 11, 12
- Joseph William Edmondson, 11, 12

Eggelton, Sarah Annie, 28
Elliott
- Fred, 49
- Jessie, 49

Evans
- Christmas, 29, 90
- Elizabeth Ann, 29
- Ivor, 90
- Ivor Morgan, 90
- Mary, 29
- Miriam Myrena, 90
- Mr. and Mrs. C., 90
- Mr. C. W., 94
- Nettie, 90
- Sergeant W. A., 4
- William Allan, 29

Everist, Major Tony, 35
Fallon
- Charlie, 67
- Ellen, 67
- Frances, 67
- Harold August (Bill), 67
- Mac, 67
- Thomas, 67
- Wes, 67

Felthan, June, 56
Filby
- Gunner T. N., 2
- Sgt. T. N., 86

Fisher, Ruby May, 65
Frankenberg
- Abraham von, 49
- Baron F. E. von, 49

French
- Grace Elizabeth, 76
- Henry Benard (Barney), 76
- Henry Stewart, 76
- Patricia Clare, 76

Freyberg, Lieutenant-General Bernard, 35
Gander
- Albert John, 44
- Horace Arthur, 39, 44
- Lucia (Lucy) Anne Daley, 44
- Mr. and Mrs. Albert, 44
- Pte. Horace A., 4

Gibson, Pte. T., 2
Godfrey, Vera Alice, 26
Goff
- Pte. James, 3
- Sapper George, 2

Goonan, Mr. J. P., 94
Gunn
- Francis Orchard, 68
- Gunner O., 3
- Orchard, 59, 73
- Valarie Helena, 68
- William George, 68

Guy, Lola, 91
Guyer, Pte. T. J., 4
Hain, Gnr. C. K., 3
Hainsworth, Vi, 56
Hal, Gunner H., 2
Hall, Sgt., 86
Hamilton, Dulcie May, 79
Hay, Pte. A, 4
Haylock
- Master Philip, 1, 3
- Mr H. C., 3

Haynes, Pte. J., 4
Healy, James, 14
Heffernan, F., 94
Heighington
- E. S., 94
- Mr. G., 94

Hewett, Leone Robert, 70
Hickey
- James, 95
- Marjorie, 95
- Miss M. W., 93
- Mr. James, 95
- Wanda, 95

Hird, Elizabeth Ann, 29
Hoar, Gnr. A., 3
Hoare, Pte. J. R., 4
Hoffmann, Sarah Elizabeth, 42
Holdsworth, Dvr. J., 86

Index

Holt, Dame Zara, 5
Homburg, Greta, 5
Hooper, E, 66
Horace Doust, 83
Hore, Percy J., 53
Horniman, Jessie Muriel, 60
Howard, Donald, 53
Howe
    Hazel Gwyneth, 88
    J, 70
Howlett, Howlett, 1
Hughes
    Gunner R., 2
    L/Bdr. R. L., 86
Hull, Pte. F. J., 3
Hunt, Mr. K. L., 94
Hurst, Maude Elizabeth, 11
Ingleton
    Miss, 94
    Mr., 94
    Mrs. I (orchestra), 94
Izzard, Gunner A. (George), 3
Jefferis, Mrs. R. E., 86
Jeffery, Susan Margret Elizabeth, 36
Jessop, Margaret (Meg), 71
Jex, Valarie Helena, 68
John Stanislaus, 41
Johnson, Miriam Myrena, 90
Jones, Mr. Charles Lloyd, 57
Kartzoff
    Michel (Mike) Eugene, 15, 16
Kelloway
    Alderman, 86
    Ald. H. S. and Mrs., 59
    Doreen Catherine, 69
    Eric George, 69
    H.S. (Mayor of Camden), 1, 3
    Horace Stanley, 69
    Minnie, 69
    Mr. and Mrs. H. S., 69, 87
    Mrs H.S., 3, 66
Kelly, Pte. W. J., 4
Kennedy, Jim, 24
Kent, George Joseph, 77
Kilpatrick, Mary M, 9
King
    Mr., 26
    Mrs. F., 62
    Mrs. Michael, 51
Kirby, Thelma, 5
Kirk, Rev. A. H., 93, 94
Lang, Mr. A. R., 94

Larnach
    Gunner R. H., 2
    Pte. K. C., 2
Lazzarini, Hubert Peter, 16
Lee
    Pte. James R., 4
    Pte. Norman, 2
Levy, Myra May, 61
Lillis, Dvr. M., 86
Lindsay, Dvr. R. C., 86
Little, Theresa, 25
Macarthur
    Joan Beatrice, 78
Macarthur, General Douglas, 38
Macarthur-Onslow
    Andrew William, 51
    Colonel Edward, 93
    Francis Arthur, 51
    Major E., 3
    Major-General J, 2
    Mr. F. A., 51
    Mrs. Sylvia, 51
    Sibella, 80
    Sylvia Seton, 51
MacIntosh, Jean Elizabeth, 54
Mackell, Lieutenant Austin, 11
Mackie, Mrs. N., 24
Maddrell, Katie May Elizabeth Coghill, 10
Malcolm
    Doreen Grace, 53
    Elsie, 53
Malony, 14
Marchant, T., 22
Marden, Pte. L. R., 86
Marriott
    Lewis Charles (Lew), 17
    Lillian Alice, 17
    Marion, 17
    Vincent Fredrick, 17
    Vivian, 17
Martin
    Captain William, 79
    Mr. G. F., 94
    Mrs. Ray, 86
Maudsley, Heather Irene, 30
Maxwell, Mr. and Mrs. M. P., 59
McGrath
    Ernest Henry, 30
    Ernest Millington, 30
    Hannah Frances, 30
    Heather Irene, 30, 31
    Mr. L. T., 94
    Pte. E. H., 4

Index

McKnight
    Alexander Andrew, 88
    Hazel Gwyneth, 88
    Keith, 88, 89
    Mary Matilda, 88
    Mr. Alex, 89
McLachlan, Mr, 31
McLeod
    Douglas John, 22
    Gordon John, 22
McPherson
    Mary Matilda, 88
McWhirter, 19
Menere, Pte. Jack, 4
Meredith, Pte. J. C., 4
Missingham, Hal (artist), 57
Moffitt
    Gnr. Clifford W., 3
    Pte. R. J., 4
Morris
    Miss Joan, 23
    Mr O., 23
Muller, Cynthia, 56
Munday, Ada Adelaide, 45
Mundell
    Samuel Cairns, 23
    William (Bill), 23
Mundle
    Ellen Agnes, 78
    George Valentine, 78
    Joan Beatrice, 78
Murdoch nee Fallon, Mrs, 67
Murdoch, Snr, Mr. J., 24
Noble, Const., 49
O'Berg, Harriette Olive, 28
O'Brien, Pte. T. W., 4
O'Neil, Will, 1
Oliver, Qtr. Sergt. A. J., 2
O'Loughlan, Driver G. J., 62
Olsen, Thelma, 5
Parker, Mrs, 36
Paterson, Cr (Nepean Shire), 12, 13
Payten
    Arthur Granville, 60
    David Rose, 60
    Jessie Muriel, 60
    Mr. and Mrs. A. G., 60
Payten, Mr. and Mrs. A. G., 60
Penfold, Henrietta Matilda, 39
Percival
    Jessie Mary, 72
    Lily, 5
Pitt-Owen Padre A. T., 31

Powell, Aircraftsman A., 3
Power, Capt. Kevin., 39
Pratt
    B. M., 94
    Gertrude, 91
    Jean Kinnear, 92
    John David, 93
    Kenneth Scott, 91
    Lola, 91
    Mary Gertrude, 92, 93
    Matthew Thomas, 91, 92, 93
    Miss Jean, 93, 94
    Miss Joan, 93
    Mr. and Mrs., 91, 93
    Mr. K. S;, 94
    Mr. R.G., 94
Price, Minnie, 69
Pry, Mr. D., 94
Putland, Rev A. E., 1
Rapley
    Edwin Morton, 70
    Gnr. E. M., 3
    Leone Robert, 70
    Mary Jane, 70
    Miss, 94
    Mrs., 70, 87
    Nita, 70
    Pte. V. N., 86
    William, 70
Readford, Ethel, 56
Reed, Pte. L., 4
Reynolds, Pte. A., 86
Richardson, Mr. Stan Richardson, 3
Rideout, Ina Jean, 22
Roberts, Jack, 24
Rona, Margaret, 15
Rose, Cr. W. Rose Cr (Nepean Shire), 12
Rudd, Cr (Nepean Shire), 12
Scholes, Sarah, 23
Scott
    Cr T. G. (Nepean Shire), 12, 13
    Gertrude, 91
    Mary Gertrude, 92, 93
Sedgwick F, 28
Segal
    Cycil, 72
    Jessie Mary, 72
    Norman Evan, 72
Sewell, Gnr. Ben G. R., 3
Shaw, Mr (Nepean Shire Clerk), 12, 13
Shepard, Miss, 24

101

Index

Sherlock
  Donald Evans, 56
  Jean, 56
Sidman
  Jean Elizabeth, 54
  Marie Celeste, 54
  Robert Alfred, 54
  William, ix
Skene
  Charles Robertson (Bob), 71
  Curtis, 71
  Elizabeth, 71
  Margaret (Meg), 71
  Mrs., 71
Skinner
  Amos Richard, 73
  Amos Roy, 73
  Maude Kathleen, 73
Small
  Mary Jane, 70
  Mrs E, 40
Smart
  Ada Adelaide, 45
  Charles Thomas, 45
  Harold William, 45
  Leta Margaret Jane, 45
  Lillian Pearl, 45
  Mr. and Mrs. C. T., 45
  Pte. O. A., 2
Smeal, Patricia Clare, 76
Smith, Mrs. Norman, 3
Spencer, Graham, 32
Spender, Mr. P. (Army Minister), 59
Stanton, Pte. Ed., 3
Stapleton, Maude Kathleen, 73
Starr
  Ainslie Plimsoll, 79
  Dulcie May, 79
  Joseph Henry, 79
  Mervyn Joseph, 79
Stephens, Capt. W. M., 61
Stevenson, Elsie Clara May, 32
Stewart
  Flying Officer Anthony, 43
  Mr J. B., 23
  Mrs M., 23
Stibbard, Mr, 86
Story, Cr (Nepean Shire), 13
Straney, Mr. S. G. (magician), 3
Stuart, Grace Elizabeth, 76
Suthers, Capt. A. G., 31
Suttle, Pte. L., 4
Suttor, Clara Mona, 26

Taplin
  Gwennyth, 25
  Mr H.V., 3
Tate
  Cecil, 25
  Colin, 25
  Gwennyth, 25
  Theresa, 25
Taylor, Mr. John, 49
Taylor, Olive Ward, 49
Thorn, P. G., 4
Thornton, Wallace (artist), 57
Timmel
  Jean Kinnear, 92
  Karl Erhard, 92
Tritton, Alfred, 62
Tyson, Jean Elizabeth, 54
Vannan, Mrs. B., 62
Varlow
  Charles Kingsley, 80
  Ella Irene, 80
  William Henry, 80
Vickers, Una Gertrude, 22
Viglione, Vinvenco, 49
Walker, Allice Elizabeth, 36
Warren nee Fallon, Mrs., 67
Watson
  Cr (Nepean Shire), 12
  Mr. R., 94
  Mrs. A. E., 62, 65
Watt, Ainslie Plimsoll, 79
Weir
  David, 56
  Ethel, 56
  Jean, 56
Wheatley
  Cr (Nepean Shire), 12, 13
  Elizabeth, 71
  Max Ian, 61, 71
  Mr. and Mrs. Roy, 61
  Myra May, 61
  Willie Roy, 61
Wheeler
  Annie Dorothy, 89
  Violet, 1
Whitehead, Sgt. Barrie, 62
Whiteley, Gunner A. L., 2
Whitton, Lieutenant Steve, 35
Wilkinson, Doreen Grace, 53
Willi, Marjorie Joan, 89

Williams
  Elsie Clara May, 32
  Enrol Wallis Stevenson, 32, 33, 34
  Mrs S. J, 32
  Rev Owen Wallis, 32
  Sapper E. C., 3
  Suzanne Jean, 32
Wills
  Clara Mona, 26
  Leonard Suttor, 26
  Percy Henry, 26
Wilmington, Mrs, 3
Wittigeustein, E, 15
Wollams, Charles, 36
Woods, Bonny, 1
Woollams
  Alice Elizabeth, 36
  Frederick Charles, 36
  Leo, 36
  Susan Margret Elizabeth, 36
Young
  Cr (Nepean Shire), 13
  Mr, 12, 26
Zglinicki, Wanda, 95

Places

Acroma, 32
Africa, 2, 37
Agricultural Hall, 1, 3, 4
Albion Park, 62, 91
Alexandria, 29
Anastasio, Camelo, 49
Appin, 61
Armidale, 65
Arncliffe, 31, 40
Ashfield, 90
Asmara, 29
Assam, 71
Auckland, 79
Austrian, 49
Baggush Box, 34
Bangkok, 73
Bankstown, 56, 76
Bardia, 14
Barrack Point, 69
Berlin, 1, 22, 25
Bethlehem, 6
Bezcouth, 29
Bomana War Cemetery, 39, 41
Borneo, 37, 62, 63, 64, 65, 91
Bougainville Is, 45
Bournemouth, 18

Bowral, 5
Bream Head, 79
Bringelly, 12, 26, 36
Britain, 2, 37, 80
Broome, 47
Burma, 37, 67, 68, 73, 90
Burwood, 26, 54, 91
Cairo, 33, 34
Camberwell, 77
Camden Museum, 22, 43, 53, 109
Camden Park, 59, 68
Camden Soldiers and Citizens' Association, 3
Campbelltown, 15, 28, 50, 54, 60, 72, 90, 92, 95
Canada, 2, 18, 25
Canal Zone, 34
Canberra, 92
Canterbury, 29
Carcoar, 91, 92
Carrington Nursing Home, 17
Cattfoss Lane, 25
Cawdor, 45, 59
Changi, 71
Charters Towers, 43
Chatswood, 10
Christchurch, 32, 34
Cobbitty, 10, 53
Cooma, 91
Cotton Tree, 80
Cowra, 93
Cranbrook, 51
Cranwell, 18
Crete, 60
Cronk Ne Voddy, 93
Crows Nest, 73
Curralubula, 51
Dalbeattie, 23
Damascus, 14
Darlinghurst, 5
Darwin, 37, 47
Dead Sea, 29
Dee Why, 80
Deniliquin, 51
Derby, 47
Doncaster, 14
Dora Creek, 80
Duchy of Oels, 49
Dunkirk, 80
Duntroon, 32, 34
Durnbach War Cemetery, Germany, 60
Dutch East Indies, 37, 47
East India, 22
East Timor, 47
Ed Duda, 34

Index

Egypt, 6, 10, 14, 32, 33, 34
El Alamein, 16, 34, 61
Elderslie, 41
England, 18, 19, 20, 25, 51, 54, 89, 93
Equator, 17
Europe, 1, 16, 37, 56, 59, 88
Exmouth Gulf, 47
Fairfield, 62
Far East, 19, 59, 70
Fiji, 17
Fort Scratchley, 48
Garden Island, 48
Gaza, 5, 6, 31
Gaza War Cemetery, 30
Germany, 1, 8, 22, 25, 37, 49, 60, 66, 89
Gilbulla, 51
Glenmore, 49
Goulburn, 61, 91
Grange, 17
Greece, 7, 14
Green Point, 47
Guma, 7
Gunnedah, 26
Haifer, 29
Harrowgate, 25
Hawaii, 37
Hawaiian Islands, 37
Honolulu, 18
Hurstville, 9
Hyde Park, 56
India, 2, 37, 71, 89, 90
Indonesia, 47
Ingleburn, 14, 51
Isle of Man, 93
Israel, 30
Italy, 16, 34, 35, 37, 56, 61
Japan, 14, 25, 37, 47, 67, 68, 69, 70, 73, 87
Java, 49, 72
Jerusalem, 5, 6, 8, 29
Jurby, 93
Kalamata, 14
Katherine, 47
Kiev, 15
Kings School, 25
Kleve, 9
Knightsbridge War Cemetery, 32
Kokoda Trail, 14
Labuan Memorial, 65
Labuan War Cemetery, 63
Lae, 44
Lae War Cemetery, 44
Leichhardt, 59, 62, 65
Libya, 14, 32, 34

Lincolnshire, 18
Liverpool, 11, 49
London, 80
Loyal Morning Star Lodge, 4
Ludwigsdorf, 49
Lybia, 11
Maadi, 34
Maaten Baggush, 34
Macarthur Park, 87
Macquarie Park Lawn Cemetery, 15
Malay, 37
Malay States, 71
Malaya, 37, 67, 71, 73
Malaysia, 63, 65
Manchester Weaving Mills, 49
Manila, 69
Margate, 20
Marrickville, 29
Mediterranean, 1, 6, 7, 16, 27, 37
Melbourne, 61, 63, 67, 76, 77
Menangle, 51, 70, 87, 91, 93, 95
Middle East, 8, 10, 14, 15, 27, 31, 34, 37, 40, 41, 44, 59, 86, 91
Millers Point, 78
Millingimbi, 47
Minnesota, 49
Moascar War Cemetery, 10
Monemein, 73
Moresby, 39
Moss Vale, 41
Mulbera, 80
Myanmar, 67, 68
Naples, 16, 29
Narellan, 14, 59, 62, 65
Nazareth, 29
Nepean Shire, 12, 13
New Guinea, 14, 39, 40, 41, 43, 44, 80, 86, 89, 91
New Zealand, 2, 32, 33, 34, 35, 79
Newcastle, 48
Nile, 6
Nordrhein-Westfalen, 9
North Africa, 1, 28, 32, 41
North Queensland, 23, 51
North Sydney, 79
Northern Territory, 47
Oakdale, 66
Orange, 30
Orangeville, 23
Oxford, 18
Pacific, 37, 43, 85, 91
Palestine, 6, 14, 16
Paris, 1
Parnell Place, 48

Parramatta, 69, 72
Pearl Harbour, 37, 47
Petersham, 30
Picton, 42, 72, 94
Poland, 89
Port Hedland, 47
Port Macquarie, 26
Port Moresby, 39, 41
Queensland, 23, 47, 92
Rabaul, 62
Randwick, 25, 44
Razorback, 70
Reichswald Forest, 9
Rhodesia, 10
Rimini, 34, 35
Rome, 71
Rossmore, 26, 36, 61
Rutherford, 23
Ryde, 67
Saigon, 73
Sandakan, 62, 63, 64
Silesia, 49
Sinai Desert, 30
Singapore, 37, 69, 71, 73
Singleton, 90
Sleaford, 18
South Australia, 25
South-West Pacific, 37
Stalag III, 89
Stalag IV, 89
Stalag XIII, 66
Stockton, 29
Stockton Beach, 48
Stuart Town, 36
Suez Canal, 6
Sulmonia, 61
Suva, 17
Switzerland, 49
Sydney, 40, 47, 48, 56, 60, 63, 73, 86
Syria, 14, 16, 34, 61
Tamworth, 51, 79
Tamworth War Cemetery, 51
Taylor Bay, 48
Tel Avin, 29
Tel Aviv, 5
Thailand, 73
Thanbyuzayat War Cemetery, 67, 68
The Oaks, 40, 59, 62
Theresa Park, 28
Tilba Tilba, 5, 6
Tobruk, 11, 14, 28, 36, 91
Tokyo, 67, 69, 70, 73
Townsville, 47, 54, 92

Tudor House, 51
Ukraine, 16
United States, 25, 37, 49
Warwick, 67
Washington, 37
Watsons Bay, 47
Waverley, 9
Wellington, 34
Werombi, 23, 67
Werriwa, 15
Western Australia, 47, 56, 72
Western Desert, 16, 32
Westmead, 79
Wewak, 14
Whangarei, 79
Wilton, 72
Woy Woy, 14
Wyndham, 47
Yass, 89
Yokohama, 73
Yorkshire, 25

Units

1 (Middle East) Training School, 10
1 Advanced Flying Unit, 93
1 Australian General Hospital (1AGH), 31
1 Australian Motor Division Signals, 90
1 Light Horse, 15
105 General Transport Company, 67
11 A.G.H., 94
113 A.G.H, 92
149 Squadron, 22
16 Garrison Battalion, 28
1668 Communications Unit, 88
18 Inf. Sng. Bn, 31
18 Infantry Battalion (NZ), 32, 34
19 Infantry Battalion (NZ), 34
2 Australian Artillery Training Regiment, 29
2 Gurkha Regiment, 71
2/1 Field Ambulance, 26
2/1 Field Company, 23
2/1 Infantry Battalion, 41
2/12 BN, 31
2/15 Field Regiment, 68, 70
2/17 Australian Infantry Battalion, 11, 91
2/2 Battalion, 14
2/2 Guard Battalion, 42
2/2 Machine Gun Battalion, 61
2/20 Australian Infantry Battalion, 63, 65
2/20 Battalion, 69
2/29 Battalion, 73
2/3 Army Field Workshops AAOC, 30, 31

Index

2/3 Battalion, 14, 36
2/3 Field Regiment, 60
2/33 Australian Infantry Battalion, 39, 44
299 Squadron, 22
2 A.I.F, 23
2 Gurkha Regiment, 71
436 Squadron (RCAF), 90
45 Battalion, 69
460 Squadron, 9
466 Squadron (UK), 89
6 Division, 14
640 Squadron, 25
7 Division, 1, 2, 37, 44
7 Service Flying Training School, 51
8 Army, 16
8 Corps of Signals, 72
8 Motor Ambulance Convoy, 26
9 Division, 15, 16, 61, 91
A.W.A.S, 56, 93
Australian Army Medical Womens Services, 43
Australian Army Salvage Section, 5
Australian Womens Army Service, 53, 56, 95
Caledonian Salvor (salvage tug), 80
Garbutt, 54
German Army, 49
HMAS Kuttabul, 48
HMAS Rushcutter, 92
HMAS Yandra, 48
HMAS Yarroma, 47
HMS Ruler, 73
K9 (Dutch submarine), 48
Koolinda, 47
Liverpool Prisoner of War & Internment Camp, 15
Middle East OCTU, 34
Montoro, 47
MV Kooringa, 77
MV Ngakuta, 78
No. 7 Recovery Section 2/3 Pioneer BN, 31
Orion (German auxiliary cruiser), 79
R.A.A.F, 3, 10, 25, 43, 51, 89, 90, 93
R.A.A.F., 18, 19, 20, 21, 52
R.A.F., 18, 20
RMS Niagara, 79
Royal Canadian Air Force, 90
Royal New South Wales Lancers, 52
SS Rona, 76
Station Laverton, 17
USS Chicago, 48
USS President Grant, 47
Voluntary Air Observer Corps, 87
W.A.A.F., 19, 20
W.R.A.N.S, 92, 94
Zealandia, 47

Bibliography

Janice relied on the following references for general discussion and context:

Camden News (NSW: 1895 - 1954) - Trove. [online] Available at: http://nla.gov.au/nla.news-title638. Digitised as part of the "Digitised newspapers and more" which allows access to historic Australian periodicals. Also available in print and on microfilm.

Camden Pioneer Register: 1800-1920 (3rd ed.). (2008). Camden, Australia: Camden Area Family History Society.

Camden Remembers. [online] Available at: http://www.camdenremembers.com.au. Records of Camden servicemen and women.

Churchill, W. (1952). *The Second World War Volume 3: The Grand Alliance:* (Reprint Society ed.).

Defence and war service records, National Archives of Australia. [online] Available at: https://www.naa.gov.au/explore-collection/defence-and-war-service-records

Johnson, Janice. *Camden's World War 1 Diggers: 1914 to 1918*. Camden Historical Society Inc, 2014.

Letters from Lewis Marriott (unpublished, held at the Camden Museum)

Roll of Honour, Australian War Memorial [online] Available at: https://www.awm.gov.au/commemoration/honour-rolls/roll-of-honour

Spencer, G. D. (1987). *The Four-legged Major*. Wellington, N.Z.: Grantham House.

World War Two Nominal Roll, Department of Veterans' Affairs [online] Available at: https://nominal-rolls.dva.gov.au/ww2

Following are the precise references to quoted articles.

[1] FAREWELL TO CAMDEN VOLUNTEERS. (1940, June 27). *Camden News (NSW: 1895 - 1954)*, p. 1. Retrieved December 30, 2020, from http://nla.gov.au/nla.news-article141147755

[2] SOLDIERS' FAREWELL. (1940, August 1). *Camden News (NSW: 1895 - 1954)*, p. 1. Retrieved December 30, 2020, from http://nla.gov.au/nla.news-article141148819

[3] PUBLIC FAREWELL. (1940, October 24). *Camden News (NSW: 1895 - 1954)*, p. 1. Retrieved December 30, 2020, from http://nla.gov.au/nla.news-article141149393

[4] LETTERS FROM SERGT, JEFF BATE, M.L.A. (1941, March 20). *Camden News (NSW: 1895 - 1954)*, p. 6. Retrieved December 29, 2020, from http://nla.gov.au/nla.news-article141149437

[5] SERGT. JEFF BATE, M.L.A. (1941, July 10). *Camden News (NSW: 1895 - 1954)*, p. 7. Retrieved December 29, 2020, from http://nla.gov.au/nla.news-article141148380

[6] Religious Services. (1945, November 1). *Camden News (NSW: 1895 - 1954)*, p. 4. Retrieved December 29, 2020, from http://nla.gov.au/nla.news-article140590244 (Note: Second paragraph in article.)

Bibliography

[7] SGT. PILOT R. F. A. DOWNES KILLED. (1942, October 15). *Camden News (NSW: 1895 - 1954)*, p. 4. Retrieved December 29, 2020, from http://nla.gov.au/nla.news-article140590303

[8] PUBLIC MEETING. (1941, October 2). *Camden News (NSW: 1895 - 1954)*, p. 1. Retrieved December 29, 2020, from http://nla.gov.au/nla.news-article141149267

[9] SERGT. MICHEL KARTZOFF. (1943, August 5). *Camden News (NSW: 1895 - 1954)*, p. 3. Retrieved December 29, 2020, from http://nla.gov.au/nla.news-article140592211

[10] WERRIWA CANDIDATE. (1943, August 12). *Camden News (NSW: 1895 - 1954)*, p. 4. Retrieved December 29, 2020, from http://nla.gov.au/nla.news-article140590889

[11] WEROMBI NEWS. (1940, January 4). *Camden News (NSW: 1895 - 1954)*, p. 1. Retrieved December 29, 2020, from http://nla.gov.au/nla.news-article141148185

[12] Roll of Honour. (1944, February 10). *Camden News (NSW: 1895 - 1954)*, p. 1. Retrieved December 29, 2020, from http://nla.gov.au/nla.news-article140590007

[13] SOCIAL AT ROSSMORE. (1940, February 29). *Camden News (NSW: 1895 - 1954)*, p. 2. Retrieved December 29, 2020, from http://nla.gov.au/nla.news-article141148134

[14] No title (1943, January 21). *Camden News (NSW: 1895 - 1954)*, p. 4. Retrieved December 29, 2020, from http://nla.gov.au/nla.news-article140590492 (Note: Last paragraph in article.)

[15] FROM THE FRONT. (1942, January 8). *Camden News (NSW: 1895 - 1954)*, p. 1. Retrieved December 29, 2020, from http://nla.gov.au/nla.news-article140586323

[16] THE LATE Pte. E. McGRATH (1941, June 26). *Camden News (NSW: 1895 - 1954)*, p. 1. Retrieved December 29, 2020, from http://nla.gov.au/nla.news-article141152927

[17] LATE PTE. E. H. McGRATH (1941, October 9). *Camden News (NSW: 1895 - 1954)*, p. 5. Retrieved December 29, 2020, from http://nla.gov.au/nla.news-article141149337

[18] Letters From the Front. (1941, March 6). *Camden News (NSW: 1895 - 1954)*, p. 3. Retrieved December 29, 2020, from http://nla.gov.au/nla.news-article141154103

[19] Churchill, Winston "The Second World War: The Grand Alliance" Volume 3 page 514

[20] THE LATE TED. BOOTH. (1944, January 20). *Camden News (NSW: 1895 - 1954)*, p. 1. Retrieved December 29, 2020, from http://nla.gov.au/nla.news-article140588173

[21] Roll of Honour. (1944, February 10). *Camden News (NSW: 1895 - 1954)*, p. 1. Retrieved December 29, 2020, from http://nla.gov.au/nla.news-article140590007

[22] DIED OF WOUNDS. (1942, December 10). *Camden News (NSW: 1895 - 1954)*, p. 1. Retrieved December 28, 2020, from http://nla.gov.au/nla.news-article140586823

[23] Roll of Honour. (1942, December 17). *Camden News (NSW: 1895 - 1954)*, p. 4. Retrieved December 28, 2020, from http://nla.gov.au/nla.news-article140587210

[24] No title (1943, April 29). *Camden News (NSW: 1895 - 1954)*, p. 2. Retrieved January 5, 2021, from http://nla.gov.au/nla.news-article140589320

[25] Roll of Honour. (1944, February 10). *Camden News (NSW: 1895 - 1954)*, p. 1. Retrieved December 28, 2020, from http://nla.gov.au/nla.news-article140590007

Bibliography

[26] No title (1945, November 1). *Camden News (NSW: 1895 - 1954)*, p. 4. Retrieved December 28, 2020, from http://nla.gov.au/nla.news-article140590247 (Note: Third item in article)

[27] Damage at Liverpool Mill. (1942, May 7). *Camden News (NSW: 1895 - 1954)*, p. 3. Retrieved December 28, 2020, from http://nla.gov.au/nla.news-article140587180

[28] BARON F. E. von FRANKENBERG. (1950, April 6). *Camden News (NSW: 1895 - 1954)*, p. 1. Retrieved December 28, 2020, from http://nla.gov.au/nla.news-article143975825

[29] No title (1943, January 21). *Camden News (NSW: 1895 - 1954)*, p. 4. Retrieved December 28, 2020, from http://nla.gov.au/nla.news-article140590492

[30] Flight Lieutenant Andrew Macarthur Onslow. (1943, February 11). *Camden News (NSW: 1895 - 1954)*, p. 1. Retrieved December 28, 2020, from http://nla.gov.au/nla.news-article140587813

[31] No title (1937, November 14). *Camden News (NSW: 1895 - 1954)*, p. 6. Retrieved January 5, 2021, from http://nla.gov.au/nla.news-article140598116

[32] J-V DAY. (1945, September 27). *Camden News (NSW: 1895 - 1954)*, p. 5. Retrieved July 17, 2021, from http://nla.gov.au/nla.news-article140588018

[33] News for Women (1949, October 20). *The Daily Telegraph (Sydney, NSW: 1931 - 1954)*, p. 16. Retrieved January 5, 2021, from http://nla.gov.au/nla.news-article248083683

[34] DIGEST OF WAR NEWS. (1941, June 19). *Camden News (NSW: 1895 - 1954)*, p. 2. Retrieved December 28, 2020, from http://nla.gov.au/nla.news-article141149352

[35] REPORTED MISSING. (1942, July 30). *Camden News (NSW: 1895 - 1954)*, p. 4. Retrieved December 28, 2020, from http://nla.gov.au/nla.news-article140586432

[36] WHEN WRITING TO PRISONERS OF WAR. (1942, August 20). *Camden News (NSW: 1895 - 1954)*, p. 3. Retrieved December 28, 2020, from http://nla.gov.au/nla.news-article140588261

[37] No title (1941, September 18). *Camden News (NSW: 1895 - 1954)*, p. 4. Retrieved December 28, 2020, from http://nla.gov.au/nla.news-article141153785

[38] No title (1941, November 27). *Camden News (NSW: 1895 - 1954)*, p. 4. Retrieved December 28, 2020, from http://nla.gov.au/nla.news-article14115324

[39] No title (1942, September 17). *Camden News (NSW: 1895 - 1954)*, p. 4. Retrieved December 28, 2020, from http://nla.gov.au/nla.news-article140590697

[40] MAJOR MAX WHEATLEY. (1944, February 10). *Camden News (NSW: 1895 - 1954)*, p. 1. Retrieved December 28, 2020, from http://nla.gov.au/nla.news-article140590000

[41] No title (1945, November 1). *Camden News (NSW: 1895 - 1954)*, p. 4. Retrieved December 28, 2020, from http://nla.gov.au/nla.news-article140590247

[42] Honour Roll. (1945, November 8). *Camden News (NSW: 1895 - 1954)*, p. 4. Retrieved December 28, 2020, from http://nla.gov.au/nla.news-article140587956

[43] Letters From the Front. (1941, March 6). *Camden News (NSW: 1895 - 1954)*, p. 3. Retrieved December 28, 2020, from http://nla.gov.au/nla.news-article141154103 (Note: Second letter)

Bibliography

[44] PRISONER OF WAR. (1941, December 11). *Camden News (NSW: 1895 - 1954)*, p. 5. Retrieved December 27, 2020, from http://nla.gov.au/nla.news-article141152813

[45] No title (1945, October 4). *Camden News (NSW: 1895 - 1954)*, p. 4. Retrieved December 27, 2020, from http://nla.gov.au/nla.news-article140592363

[46] DEATH OF Pte. BILL FALLON (1945, June 28). *Camden News (NSW: 1895 - 1954)*, p. 4. Retrieved December 27, 2020, from http://nla.gov.au/nla.news-article140585902

[47] No title (1944, August 17). *Camden News (NSW: 1895 - 1954)*, p. 4. Retrieved December 27, 2020, from http://nla.gov.au/nla.news-article140591619

[48] No title (1943, June 24). *Camden News (NSW: 1895 - 1954)*, p. 2. Retrieved December 27, 2020, from http://nla.gov.au/nla.news-article140586895

[49] No title (1944, April 13). *Camden News (NSW: 1895 - 1954)*, p. 2. Retrieved December 27, 2020, from http://nla.gov.au/nla.news-article140592636

[50] GENERAL INFORMATION (1945, September 20). *Camden News (NSW: 1895 - 1954)*, p. 1. Retrieved December 27, 2020, from http://nla.gov.au/nla.news-article140587328

[51] No title (1943, October 14). *Camden News (NSW: 1895 - 1954)*, p. 2. Retrieved December 26, 2020, from http://nla.gov.au/nla.news-article140587413

[52] No title (1945, September 20). *Camden News (NSW: 1895 - 1954)*, p. 2. Retrieved December 26, 2020, from http://nla.gov.au/nla.news-article140587342

[53] Religious Services. (1945, October 11). *Camden News (NSW: 1895 - 1954)*, p. 4. Retrieved December 26, 2020, from http://nla.gov.au/nla.news-article140589832. (Note: The article is not indexed by Trove, the article is in the same column and follows this reference.)

[54] "PRISONERS OF WAR ADOPTION SCHEME." *Camden News (NSW: 1895 - 1954)* 21 January 1943: 4. Web. 26 Dec 2020 <http://nla.gov.au/nla.news-article140590490>. (Note: The article is not indexed by Trove, the article is in the column immediate to the left of this reference and down an inch or so.)

[55] News From P.O.W. (1944, May 25). *Camden News (NSW: 1895 - 1954)*, p. 5. Retrieved December 26, 2020, from http://nla.gov.au/nla.news-article140586289

[56] LETTER FROM TOKYO. (1945, September 27). *Camden News (NSW: 1895 - 1954)*, p. 1. Retrieved December 26, 2020, from http://nla.gov.au/nla.news-article140588021

[57] No title (1945, October 4). *Camden News (NSW: 1895 - 1954)*, p. 4. Retrieved December 26, 2020, from http://nla.gov.au/nla.news-article140592363

[58] Letters from the Front. (1941, March 20). *Camden News (NSW: 1895 - 1954)*, p. 6. Retrieved December 26, 2020, from http://nla.gov.au/nla.news-article141149453

[59] THE AFTERMATH OF WAR. (1946, October 24). *Camden News (NSW: 1895 - 1954)*, p. 5. Retrieved December 25, 2020, from http://nla.gov.au/nla.news-article140493794

[60] THANKSGIVING. (1945, October 4). *Camden News (NSW: 1895 - 1954)*, p. 1. Retrieved December 25, 2020, from http://nla.gov.au/nla.news-article140592359

[61] SOLDIERS' WELCOME. (1944, February 24). *Camden News (NSW: 1895 - 1954)*, p. 5. Retrieved December 25, 2020, from http://nla.gov.au/nla.news-article140588385

[62] THESE AGONISING WEEKS. (1945, September 20). *Camden News (NSW: 1895 - 1954)*, p. 1. Retrieved December 25, 2020, from http://nla.gov.au/nla.news-article140587330

[63] WELCOME HOME. (1945, October 11). *Camden News (NSW: 1895 - 1954)*, p. 1. Retrieved December 25, 2020, from http://nla.gov.au/nla.news-article140589818

[64] Religious Services. (1945, October 11). *Camden News (NSW: 1895 - 1954)*, p. 4. Retrieved December 25, 2020, from http://nla.gov.au/nla.news-article140589832 (note: the article is two paragraphs down, but not indexed by Trove)

[65] Distinguished Flying Cross. (1945, February 1). *Camden News (NSW: 1895 - 1954)*, p. 2. Retrieved January 12, 2021, from http://nla.gov.au/nla.news-article140588598

[66] R.S.S. & A.I.L.A. (1945, November 8). *Camden News (NSW: 1895 - 1954)*, p. 1. Retrieved January 12, 2021, from http://nla.gov.au/nla.news-article140587953

[67] No title (1945, August 2). *Camden News (NSW: 1895 - 1954)*, p. 4. Retrieved December 25, 2020, from http://nla.gov.au/nla.news-article140590642

[68] Religious Services. (1945, October 11). *Camden News (NSW: 1895 - 1954)*, p. 4. Retrieved December 25, 2020, from http://nla.gov.au/nla.news-article140589832 (note: the article is three paragraphs down, but not indexed by Trove)

[69] Religious Services. (1945, November 1). *Camden News (NSW: 1895 - 1954)*, p. 4. Retrieved December 25, 2020, from http://nla.gov.au/nla.news-article140590244 (note: the article is four paragraphs down, but not indexed by Trove)

[70] MENANGLE NEWS. (1945, November 15). *Camden News (NSW: 1895 - 1954)*, p. 1. Retrieved December 25, 2020, from http://nla.gov.au/nla.news-article140590203

[71] MENANGLE NEWS. (1945, November 15). *Camden News (NSW: 1895 - 1954)*, p. 1. Retrieved December 25, 2020, from http://nla.gov.au/nla.news-article140590203

[72] MENANGLE NEWS. (1946, June 13). *Camden News (NSW: 1895 - 1954)*, p. 2. Retrieved December 25, 2020, from http://nla.gov.au/nla.news-article140492246

[73] MENANGLE NEWS. (1937, March 18). *Camden News (NSW: 1895 - 1954)*, p. 5. Retrieved December 25, 2020, from http://nla.gov.au/nla.news-article140596962

www.ingramcontent.com/pod-product-compliance
Lightning Source LLC
Chambersburg PA
CBHW061536010526
44107CB00066B/2883